T0128359

# RAMBLING THOUGHTS

*By*

Thomas G. Roberts

Order this book online at www.trafford.com
or email orders@trafford.com

Most Trafford titles are also available at major online book
retailers.

© Copyright 2010 Thomas G. Roberts.
All rights reserved. No part of this publication may be reproduced,
stored in a retrieval system, or transmitted, in any form or by
any means, electronic, mechanical, photocopying, recording, or
otherwise, without the written prior permission of the author.

Printed in the United States of America.

ISBN: 978-1-4120-3405-0 (sc)

ISBN: 978-1-4122-2621-9 (e-book)

*Our mission is to efficiently provide the world's finest,
most comprehensive book publishing service, enabling
every author to experience success. To find out how to
publish your book, your way, and have it available
worldwide, visit us online at www.trafford.com*

*Trafford rev. 6/29/2010*

 www.trafford.com

North America & international
toll-free: 1 888 232 4444 (USA & Canada)
phone: 250 383 6864 ♦ fax: 812 355 4082

# Prologue

A dear friend, who is a devout Baptist that believes in a literal interpretation of the Bible, (his English translation that is) is genuinely worried about my not being saved. He, of course, believes in salvation through faith alone. It bothers him that so many people, who don't otherwise deserve to get in, will do so through faith and precious little else, while others like myself, whom he considers to be of a high moral character, will end up in hell because of a lack of faith. He can understand from his Bible how we came to be here, why we are here, how long we will be here, and what will happen to us in a little over 200 years when all of this comes to an end. He understands the "true" meanings of the events in creation, the events that transpired at the crucifixion, and the events that are described in Revelation. He understands these in a fuller and deeper way than the preachers and theologians with whom he has conversed. If you will accept that every word in the Bible is the word of God, then he can and does make a strong argument to support his position. Moreover he feels that Christianity is the only religion that gives justification for existence. He made a list of questions that he could answer from the Christian viewpoint. The answers to these questions are his raison d'etre (reason or justification for existence). He wanted me to try to answer these questions as a non-believer or a believer in some other religion would answer them.

I knew that he was motivated by his desire to convince me that his answers were so much better than anything that I might find elsewhere and thereby convince me that I had better become a Christian again. I say again, because I was and as far as the church is concerned, I still am a member. However, it is the Episcopalian Church and not The Baptist. Even so, this made him feel much better. For him, heaven is or will be populated by all Christians, not just the Baptist. He genuinely believes that I will be there in spite of myself. Let's hope and pray that this is correct, if his other believes are correct.

I told him that I don't argue religion with anyone, and as far as I know he is the only one (outside my family) with whom I will discuss it. He said that he did not want to argue about any answers that I might find. He only wanted to know what they were, in order to help him with the preparation of the presentation of his interpretation of the Bible. I reluctantly agreed to give the questions some thought. His questions were worded to enlist answers from the Christian dogma. I felt that to address each question separately would tend to promote arguments. Therefore, I decided to answer all of his questions by writing what I really believe about our raison d'entre (reason for being).

Since I did not know at the time what I really believed, I was not sure where to start. I had recently read all of the Story of Civilization by Will and Ariel Durant, all twelve volumes including The Lessons of History. I then read the Collected Writings of Thomas Paine. After reading these books, it was possible to start without a bias for any particular religion, except possibly that of a Deist. I decided to start with just the central question and let inspiration be my guide. Milton Howie who caused me to address this question inspired the following writings.

Shortly after I started this writing, the following cartoons were printed in The Huntsville Times. I made copies and gave them to Milton as my first response to his questions. The second response follows.

I have tried not to be recondite. That is, I have tried to be as clear and as simple as possible, which should be easy for me.

## Peanuts

PEANUTS reprinted by permission of United Feature Syndicate, Inc.

PEANUTS reprinted by permission of United Feature Syndicate, Inc.

## Non Sequitur

Non Sequitur ©2003 Wiley Miller. Dist. by Universal Press Syndicate. Reprint with
permission. All rights reserved.

# Contents

# Rambling Thoughts

What do I really believe or what is our (raison d'etre) reason or justification for existence?

Most people look to religion (that is faith) for the answer and this determines it for them. Although thinking beings are born with no cognizance of religion, they are taught religion or the lack of it by their parents and the society in which they are raised. Therefore, all people are born with a free will, that is they are free to believe in any of the existing religions, any of the previously existing religions, no religion at all, make up one of their own, or modify one of the existing religions so that it is close to the actual teaching of its founders and thus become a pariah (outcast). Very few if any get a chance to exercise this free will except in a very highly biased manner. Also a belief in one religion generally requires non-belief in all the others, and therefore, discourages even learning about or trying to understand them much less accepting any one or more of them.

How is it then that some reject the religion that they are born into and accept some other religion, no religion at all, or attempt to make up a new one? It is because they are inattentive, poor learners, astute observers, born skeptics, natural free thinkers or as more generally happens, they are coerced by conquering peoples of another religion, by economic considerations, or marriage. Nearly everyone has some empathy, sympathy, or understanding of most of these people.

But, what about the poor pathetic soul who in the exercise of his free will cannot bring himself to accept one religion over all the others, accept all the religions as being equally valid or useful, and cannot be satisfied with no religion at all, and then attempts to make up a new one? Doesn't he know that the new religion must give a raison d'etre that is different from the others and hopefully more satisfying? To attempt to make up a new religion is a very daunting task. How would one go about it?

First it must be realized that there is a tremendous difference between making up a religion and creating or founding a religion. A made up religion may have as few as one believer. To create a religion you must have enough faithful believers so that the results of their actions which results from following this faith causes others to reject their current status and convert to the new faith; thus, producing a large enough following to cause some effect (which is hopefully good and lasting) on the history of civilization. It should also be realized that the task might not be completed. Never start expecting or even hoping at some point to say, "Eureka, I have found it", just be hopeful to at some point to obtain some form of acceptable closure.

I think that all people believe that GOD is a good word, which may be spelled and pronounced in different ways in different times and places. However, some believe that it does not have a plural form and others believe that it has no meaning. I hope this paper turns out to be of interest to all three groups, especially the last one.

What to do next? We could study the history of other religions to see what they have in common and what are their primary differences, to learn how they were born, grew, and if they are extinct why they died. We could study the history of civilization to learn the effects of religion on its development. Fortunately, this has been done quite well for us by Will and Ariel Durant and is summarized in the little book "The Lessons of History". Chapter VII of the Lessons of History, entitled Religion and History is enclosed here for background and reference material.

# EXTRACT FROM
# LESSONS OF HISTORY

## Chapter VII.  Religion and History
*By*

*Will and Ariel Durant*

In spite of several efforts to obtain permission to reproduce the copyrighted material in Chapters VII, VI and III of *The Lessons of History*, I have been unable to do so.

The following is a copy of the letter that was sent to the Will and Ariel Durant Foundation:

*"Dear Madam/Sir:*

*I have used three chapters from The Lessons of History in a work that I called "Rambling Thoughts on Raison d'entre (The Reason for Existing or the Meaning of it All)." I am not a professional author. I have written many scientific reports, papers, books and 70 patents. However, these works were not offered for sale. The above work is not a scholarly effort in that there are no footnotes and references are given only when I could remember them. There are no chapters and the work has not been edited in the sense that I have tried to not go back and change anything. I wanted to leave it just as the thought came to me.*

*Having been raised a Christian; I felt that the results of this work would only cause troubles with my Christian friends. Therefore, I wanted my wife to see if it was worth publishing only after I had passed on. Of course, an author generally thinks more of his work than anyone else would and it has been my experience that if the work is out of the field of his expertise or training, he is most likely suffering from an illusion.*

*Keeping these facts in mind, I would like to get an independent opinion and since most of my thoughts come from reading 'The Story of Civilization". I would value your opinion most of all – regardless of what that opinion may be.*

*As you will see, I have made an attempt to write so that the three chapters from "The Lessons of History" could be omitted, but for me, this would be a big loss.*

*I have also written an autobiography for my descendants, entitled "One of the Innumerable Stories that Generally remains Untold (Primarily for my Children and Grandchildren)." If you will allow me, I would like to send you a copy of these two works for your review. The biography is included so that you might understand the background of the author of "Rambling Thoughts" - that is seeing where I came from.*

*I apologize for the length of this message, but when I am asking for a lot, I felt an explanation was necessary. Your response is graciously requested."*

It is not reasonable to expect each reader to buy a copy of *The Lessons of History,* however, if you were to be exiled to an uninhabited tropical island and you could only take one book with you, and then let that book be *The Story of Civilization by Will and Ariel Durant.*

# Resume Rambling Thoughts

SEQUITUR: The conclusions of an inference: Consequence.

(1) Religion has been seemingly indispensable in every land and age. In the case of communism, communism itself becomes a religion.

(2) A moral code of some sort has always been indispensable.

(3) GOD or GODS are not always necessary. Religions have been created without them.

(4) Religion at first does not seem to have any connection with morals. Apparently it was fear that made GODS necessary. They were needed for protection and support.

(5) Morals were and are needed to allow beings to interact with one another in a cooperative and somewhat peaceful manner.

(6) To make morals effective, there has to be some form of punishment for disobedience. This is one of the functions of governments and civil laws.

(7) It works best if some of these punishments are backed up by supernatural laws, i.e. the laws of the GODS.

(8) Thus, it is when the "priest" uses the fears that produced the GODS and the rituals that placate them to support morality and the law that religion becomes a force vital for governing people. Of course, this does not mean that the "priest" becomes or remains moral. Also, the prospect of both fears of punishment for disobedience and reward received for obedience work best.

(9) The priest would like to rule the spiritual and the secular and both by divine right. But, theocracies don't seem to last

or grow due to a necessary loss of freedom and persecuting non-believers.

(10) When the civil government became secularized, the priest then wants to rule the spiritual and to stand between the state and the GODS, thereby sanctioning the civil rule (by divine right). In return the civil rule protects the state religion against other religions.

(11) Religion now brings to the people, especially the poor people, super-natural comforts that are more precious than anything else. It gives them dignity, and enables them to tolerate suffering and oppression. It also keeps them from killing the rich.

(12) There are now cases where the state is divorced from religion. That is, there is no state religion. This works quite well when religious tolerance is guaranteed. The state has to not only with-hold aid from all religions, but it also has to keep them from killing each other.

(13) Cases (like communism and most, if not all Utopias) where there is no religious tolerance, and the state takes the place of religion, generally don't last or they change so as to permit religions to exist if not flourish.

To make up a religion do we really need to create a GOD? It seems that this is sufficient, but not necessary. For example, Buddha did not need one, but his followers later created one. Never the less, nearly all are begun by someone creating a GOD or GODS. These GODS have had many different forms, properties and power. Many of the early Greek and later Roman GODS were given human or human-like forms. The Hebrew people make their GOD to be autonomous, mystic, and all powerful and then, if you can believe it, they let this GOD make man in his own image. However, at that time he was GOD of only a small, insignificant, tribe, which had essentially no power and little else, so you see it doesn't take much to make a GOD. This part of the task could be easy, but probably will be much more difficult than it sounds. Also, GOD or GODS once created don't remain the same. Some of them fight each other and even kill or eliminate one another, and may then assume the powers of the vanquished.   Other GODS let their people fight each other and in this manner determine which GODS are most fit for survival.  Some GODS evolve by the creation of religions that instead of creating a new GOD simply adopt or change in some way an existing or previous GOD or GODS to make "HIM" different.  This happens when an existing GOD is adopted by people, (other than those who created the GOD) and then change "HIM" to suit their needs?  This was done by the followers of Buddha and by the people who took their version of the teachings of James and his brother Jesus to the Gentiles and by Moham-mad when he created the Islamic Religion.  The Jewish Christians added a loving nature to the vengeful war-like nature of the Hebrew GOD and to entice the Gentiles they created the Trinity while maintaining monotheism. Things that seem to be oxymoronic to us don't have to be contradictory to the GODS or The GOD.

Did any of the extinct GODS exist and do any of the extant GODS really exist?  Yes, they all existed and all of the current ones exist today.  They ex-isted at a minimum, in the minds of their believers.  To them at least, they were real.  It is good that this is true because they were and are necessary. This is what caused Voltaire to say, "If GOD did not exist, then it would be necessary for us to invent 'Him'."  This will probably always be the case, however, at some time in the infinite future, there may occur a time when all people here on earth have the same GOD and brotherhood, love, and peace will become a reality.   At this time we may have to face the problems caused by phenomena beyond the earth.  If the former occurs first, we will be ready for the latter. More about this later.

Since so many GODS have been created, it shouldn't be so difficult to make up one more.  But where do you start?  Why not start, "In the begin-ning"?  Do we really know that there ever was a beginning or for that matter will there be an end?  It seems to us that all things have a beginning and an end, so why shouldn't creation?  If creation had a beginning, who or what did it and how was it done?  This is where GOD, as a rule, first comes into play, and "He" must be given the powers necessary to create and to rule what "He" creates.  In our case let's start by assuming that GOD is infinitely infinite.

Infinite has several definitions, but all of them mean beyond the comprehension of man.  Well now, does that mean we are going to make up a GOD or GODS that we can't know anything about?  Of course not, men know a great deal about several things that are infinite. Yet they know really nothing of their ultimate limits.  One of the best examples of this is our number system.  The integers are infinite (no one comprehends the largest one).  The rational fractions are also infinite, but even though they contain the integers, they are of the same size as the integers.  The irrational numbers are those fractions, which are not contained in the rational numbers. That is why we call them irrational.  These irrational numbers are also infinite, and are the same size as the rational numbers.  When we take the rational plus the irrational numbers we obtain a set of real numbers, a set that is infinitely larger, than either the rational or irrational numbers. Even though the real numbers are infinitely larger, they are only twice as large.  You see, we count, one infinity, two infinity, etc.  It is not necessary to define the complex numbers here, but if I did, we would find that they are infinitely larger than the real numbers, so that we now have one infinity, two infinity, three infinity; and it is possible to continue.

Thus, even though we cannot comprehend everything about the numbers, we can still understand some of their properties and know ways to use them so that they tell us a lot about their nature.  The same can be said about space, time, matter, GODS, and other infinite concepts.

Can this GOD, who is infinitely infinite, help us explain or understand evolution as we sense it today?  Can GOD talk to us, and if so how?  Can we understand how GOD created life, that is, what he did when he created it? Can GOD help us to predict the future or part of it?  Can GOD help us to understand the difference between good and evil and help us to develop a useful moral code?  The answer is YES!  GOD has been, is doing, and will continue to do these things and much more.  Of course, we will never know more than a finite amount.  (There will always be more than we know, no matter how much we learn.)  If we begin to think that we may be getting near to knowing most that there is to know about GOD we will be fooling ourselves.  More about all of this later, but let me warn you, when GOD talks to us; he talks to all of us and not to a chosen one or a chosen few. Although, there may be times when this seems to be the case.

Currently, when one tries to imagine how things may have begun, if they had a beginning at all, he turns to cosmology. He tries to make up a plausible model that is as consistent as, possible with, the laws of physics, as we know them today. There is no certainty that there is only one unique model that may do this, and we cannot design an experiment, establish initial conditions and run a check on the predictability of our chosen model except in a very small space in the neighborhood of our solar system. Therefore, even though we do cosmology as scientifically as we can, cosmology still lacks the most outstanding characteristic of a science, which is the certainty of predictability. Cosmology is an exercise of the imagination. The most accepted model produced by this exercise is the so-called, Big Bang, which requires everything in the universe to, at one time, to have been contained in a very small volume. There is no understanding of how it came to be that way or how long it took to come to be that way. But, it must have been in a state of dynamic unstable equilibrium, until some perturbation (GOD?) caused it to break equilibrium, and explode in an extreme manner. Since this small dot contained everything (all the matter and energy) it was also very hot. Thus, as it expanded it cooled and dynamically formed everything we are able to sense today and maybe much more. I didn't say that cosmology would not be tough on the imagination; but you can imagine anything you want. We sense this expansion by measuring the Doppler shift of the spectral radiation reaching the earth from distant sources. This also lets us determine how far away these sources are, and when the radiation was born. This gives us a lower limit on the age of the universe. This may be getting a little involved for the average reader, but it is a brief description of how cosmology is played. Why is cosmology important? First it helps explain how the Milky Way, our sun, the planets, and especially the Earth came into being and if we are going to consider GOD as the creator, we would like our GOD to be at least consistent with the model. We would also like for him to be able to be consistent with any other possible model that may be developed. That is we don't want our understanding of this and/or any other thing to contradict our GOD or cast doubt on "HIS" existence.

Are there any other plausible models? Well, let's try to make one up, and let's try to be as logical as we can. First, let's assume that everything has to be somewhere. Then when there is only one thing it can be anywhere (the case of the big band), or it can be everywhere. Which is the case we will take, since it is different from the Big Bang? In both cases we start when this thing is in a state of unstable dynamic equilibrium. In either case there is no such thing as time until the equilibrium is broken. Our case is something like constrained steady state magnetohydrodynamic motion. Now at some time, say zero time, something (like GOD or GODS) releases or breaks the constraints causing the flowing matter, which contained an astronomical (if not infinite) amount of energy, to become highly non-linear. The non-linearity creates swirls that collect extremely large (but finite) amounts of matter into domains. In doing this, empty or nearly empty (Dark Matter?) space is created between the domains. Most of the volume of the universe is now filled by the space between the domains. These first domains will later become known as a cluster of a cluster of galaxies. Then these first domains break up into a number of small domains each of which becomes a cluster of galaxies. Still later these small domains break up into yet smaller domains, which become galaxies, and so on until the suns and their solar systems are formed.

This is only the beginning of this model, the picture we have so far is very simplistic, but it is really much more complicated than the Big Bang. The set of non-linear magnetohydrodynamic equation required for this model may not even be imagined (at this time) much less solved, which greatly limits the usefulness of such a model. We would also have to address such things as the Doppler Effect. In this case it would be easy to take advantage of the imaginative nature of cosmology. We would just assume that all of space is filled with dark matter or celestial ether, which has a complex index of refraction. That is, it interacts with electromagnetic radiation to change the energy of a photon as a function of time or distance. Now all we have to do is calculate the required properties of this dark matter and then to try to convince ourselves that it really is there. Enough of this nonsense, it was only used to show the nature of cosmology. If we were to find out that electromagnetic radiation really does get tired (lose energy) in traveling a long way, you can be sure that the cosmologist won't close up shop and go away. They will just change their model to include this affect, or find a new one. (See continuation of this discussion in the Appendix A.)

Let's get back to our new GOD and see what we can learn about "Him" or "His" ways. We are going to help the cosmologist (and my mental well being) by assuming that even GOD does not make something out of nothing. He made everything out of something, that thing which existed, "In the beginning --". Let's start with in the beginning was the word, the word was with GOD, and the word was GOD. What does this mean? It means that in the beginning there was GOD, only GOD and nothing else. Then it is clear that GOD made everything out of himself! Everything that exists is part of GOD! Everything was made in GOD'S image. In a sense I like that; I am part of GOD; I am GOD'S son. But then so too are the bugs, worms, germs, the animals, dirt, gold, slime and etc. I had better not let this go to my head and I had better look upon other things both animals and inanimate objects in a different light for they too are part of GOD. From this we should learn how to react with and treat all things. We might even learn what's good and what's evil. That is what is good from bad. More about this later, but first let's consider life.

When did GOD create life and how did he do it? Without going into details about what GOD has told us, so far, about nuclear physics and atomic physics, we will start with the atoms. You see GOD not only talks to us but he does it over and over and over, so that we may eventually hear him and learn part of what is being said. When GOD made the atoms, which may be a continuous or possibly a recurring process, he made them with valence electrons. It is the physics of these valence electrons that explains all of chemistry, as we now know it. The valence electrons cause the atoms to make molecules, crystals, and other forms. The code that is instructions for doing this, and the need to do these things is contained in the energies of valence electrons. Thus, when conditions are right, the molecules, crystals and other forms will just happen. A subset of this chemistry, called hydrocarbon chemistry, allows organic molecules to form. These molecules, using the residual information contained in them, to form organisms both plant and animal.  When GOD made hydrocarbon chemistry he made life in all of its possible forms, and given enough time, life will occur whenever conditions are appropriate for it to do so.  Most stars (suns) don't have satellites, but many do.  About each sun there is a zone where life could exist.  Let's call this zone the life zone.  If there is a planet in this zone, then it is neither to close to the sun to make it too hot for life nor too far away to be too cold for life.  The planet must also be neither too big nor too small.  The planet must be big enough to hold an atmosphere that can sustain life, but not so large that gravity could prevent it.  The planet and its atmosphere must also contain water.  You can see that these conditions will rarely be met.  Never the less, there are so many suns that these conditions will most likely be found in a very large number of places.  In each of these places, life will be found.  This is one of the things that GOD tells us.  GOD'S laws are constant in time and space.  The life that exists in these far away places may be quite different from that here on Earth, but there will be more similarities that there will be differences.  Hydrocarbon chemistry just works that way.  GOD has told us (shown us) that material things must travel at a finite velocity that is less than the speed of light.  Therefore, there is no such thing as aliens from outer space, and Earthlings will not visit life on other worlds.  It is also foolish for us to try to communicate with life on other worlds.  We don't know where the worlds are and we cannot afford to broadcast into 4 π steer-radians.  This would require an output power something like or exceeding that of our sun.  Neither, does it make sense for us to expect that beings from other worlds are trying to communicate with us; unless, we assume that they are much further advanced than we are and somehow can sense where we are. If such an advanced culture did exist it should be able to perform feats undreamed of by us.  They would also realize how backward we are and would do something that would be easy for us to detect.  Something like modulating a binary star! It may seem egotistical but considering how well the human race has evolved and how well we have been able to interpret what GOD has been telling us, I feel that we may be close to one of the most advanced civilizations that exist.  However, it is also strikingly clear that we have come only a small part of the journey. We will have to keep listening to GOD and interpret much more before there will be peace on Earth and a complete understanding for the rights of man. Will there ever be a time when a philosopher may set foot anywhere on Earth and say, "this is my country"? Perhaps that will be when the meek shall inherit the Earth. But first, we must realize that each of us is a son (or daughter) of GOD and treat each other as such.

As we have seen having a GOD and having a religion are two different things and having a moral code is different yet. These things don't necessarily come packaged together. What has history taught us about these things? Fortunately, Will and Ariel Durant have summarized part of this for us in Chapter VI on Morals and History and this chapter is included here for background and reference material.

# EXTRACT FROM LESSONS OF HISTORY

## Chapter VI.  Morals and History

*By*
*Will and Ariel Durant*

In spite of several efforts to obtain permission to reproduce the copyrighted material in Chapters VII, VI and III of *The Lessons of History*, I have been unable to do so.

The following is a copy of the letter that was sent to the Will and Ariel Durant Foundation:

*"Dear Madam/Sir:*

*I have used three chapters from The Lessons of History in a work that I called "Rambling Thoughts on Raison d'entre (The Reason for Existing or the Meaning of it All)."  I am not a professional author.  I have written many scientific reports, papers, books and 70 patents.  However, these works were not offered for sale.  The above work is not a scholarly effort in that there are no footnotes and references are given only when I could remember them.  There are no chapters and the work has not been edited in the sense that I have tried to not go back and change anything.  I wanted to leave it just as the thought came to me.*

*Having been raised a Christian; I felt that the results of this work would only cause troubles with my Christian friends.  Therefore, I wanted my wife to see if it was worth publishing only after I had passed on.  Of course, an author generally thinks more of his work than anyone else would and it has been my experience that if the work is out of the field of his expertise or training, he is most likely suffering from an illusion.*

*Keeping these facts in mind, I would like to get an independent opinion and since most of my thoughts came from reading 'The Story of Civilization". I would value your opinion most of all – regardless of what that opinion may be.*

*As you will see, I have made an attempt to write so that the three chapters from "The Lessons of History" could be omitted, but for me, this would be a big loss.*

*I have also written an autobiography for my descendants, entitled "One of the Innumerable Stories that Generally remains Untold (Primarily for my Children and Grandchildren)." If you will allow me, I would like to send you a copy of these two works for your review. The biography is included so that you might understand the background of the author of "Rambling Thoughts" - that is seeing where I came from.*

*I apologize for the length of this message, but when I am asking for a lot, I felt an explanation was necessary. Your response is graciously requested."*

It is not reasonable to expect each reader to buy a copy of *The Lessons of History,* however, if you were to be exiled to an uninhabited tropical island and you could only take one book with you; then let that book be *The Story of Civilization by Will and Ariel Durant.*

# Resume Rambling Thoughts

MORALS - to kill or not to kill that is the question? Is it noble in the minds of men to prove (through conquest and the accumulation of power) that your group's virtue is the only correct one, even though this involves killing? Killing, by the religion, the state or both, for this purpose, obviously makes killing a virtue. Once this course is adopted, which seems to have happened before the time of recorded history, man soon learns that "Haunts" really do exist. If you have a chance to kill an enemy, and don't do it, then the enemy will come back to haunt you. Killing seems to be a virtue when survival, security, or the maintenance of power depends on it. Even today we sometimes consider killing a virtue and make efficient killers heroes. Consider the Flying Aces of WWI and WWII, the bomber crews, Jimmy Dolittle, the crew of the Enola Gay, Audi Murphy, George S. Patton, etc. etc. and etc. It seems that killing is either good or bad depending on whether it hinders or promotes the control of the people and on who wins.

The above discussions tend to indicate why religions generally don't come with a moral code. The moral code of the Hebrew people does not come until the time of Moses, many eons after Adam and Eve. Until this time, they were to believe in one GOD and only one GOD and to do as he says to them either personally or through prophets. Then HE would protect them and make them prosper. If they did not believe, then he was vengeful and would make them suffer. Both of these things were to happen here on Earth, not in a heaven or a hell. During this time, if GOD told them to go out and conquer some land by killing all of the people; men, women and children, then they knew that if they had been truly faithful, they would be able to do this, and it would be the moral thing to do. But, if they had not been faithful, then they would fail and many (supposedly the unfaithful) would be killed, and all their children for four generations would suffer for their sins. It seems that this too was moral. It was also during this time that GOD either killed or had killed the first-born child of all of the Egyptians and this too was moral.

When GOD gave Moses the Ten Commandments, the Hebrew people had a moral code. Here it may have been better had one of the commandments said thou should not commit murder so that it could be distinguished from killing. Killings would be those sanctioned by the GOD, the religion, or the state or whoever has the power to sanction. Note that the first commandment says that you are either in or you are out, and until years after the time of Christ, this applied only to the Israelites. Everyone else was out.

It is not going to be easy to discover (arrive at) the moral code that is being taught by our new GOD. This GOD is new only in the sense that we are just now trying to recognize or understand "HIM". He has been and will be here forever and ever. It never has been easy, but it is much easier when the code can be handed down from the supernatural GOD through some governing authority to the people being governed. So that the government can include those things which help make the people easy to control and to forbid those things, which do otherwise.

It would be nice if we could adopt the dualism of ZOROASTRIAN or MANICHAEAN. That is, a battle between a good spirit (GOD and Heaven) and an evil spirit (the Devil and hell) for the control of the universe and men's souls. But, we must be very careful not to force the good spirit and the evil spirit to fit our preconceived notions. We must try to just let them turn out however they may; even if this means that only one of the spirits survives or that many more are needed. There is no chance that there will be less than one, for we already have one, and that is our own creator.

Let's see what kind of trouble we can get into if we are not very careful. GOD created everything, but the only place where we can make close up observations is here on Earth. One observation is that for everything created, plant or animal, there was also created one or more predators. How can this be? What about the number one predator? Who or what is its Predator? First, let's look at the insects. They have one major predator, the spider. The spider controls the population of the insects, which is a blessing for man and the other animals. It seems that GOD created the spiders for this purpose, but what is the predator of the spider? What controls their population?  The spider has several predators but only one effective one, and that is the spiders themselves.  (The housewife is an almost negligible predator but she still comes in second.)  When the spiders reduce the insect level and reproduce to increase their level so that food for them becomes short, they then kill one another until the insect level is again slightly over populated and the cycle repeats itself.  Likewise, man plays the part of the spider for all of the other animals.  Man is also the major predator for all of the natural and renewable resources available on Earth.  Who is supposed to be man's major predator?  Of course, it is man himself.  Man is to control his population through what ever means necessary.  It seems that this was first accomplished by difficulties involved in providing food and sometimes in killing people who tried to share or take over your hunting grounds.  Later on, when food could be cultivated, a larger population could be sustained except in the times of famine when starvation and wars for food supplies help keep the populations down.  A state of war seems to have been a continuous and a natural condition for most of man's existence.  For example, when America was discovered, the natives had no concept of peace as we speak of it today.  They had always been in a state of conflict with their neighbors.

If we make the mistake of trying to cast this in the dualism of good and evil to arrive at a moral code, then we would make the creator GOD and it would be good and natural to do whatever is necessary to control the human population and to limit it to a level that allows our renewable resources to sustain us for a nearly unlimited time.  Carbon fuels are exhaustible and we are using them up at an alarmingly increasing rate.  We use much of this fuel to make fertilizer and other chemicals, which allows us to feed what seems to be an ever-increasing population.

At the increasing rate at which we are using these fuels, the carbon fuel era will be just a very narrow blip (spectral line) on a linear plot in time. How did this come about and what do we do about the Devil?  Is the Devil responsible for this?  What if, sometime ago, say about 2000 years ago, the Devil decided that the best way to defeat GOD was to convince man that he should not be his own worst predator; that men should love one another, even love their enemies, to turn the other cheek, and to not kill, but only put up a passive resistance, and to make those who do kill ashamed of himself.

To accomplish man's self-destruction of man he sent his son (the Devil's advocate) to Earth to teach love of man for man and to replace killing with devotion to a loving deity.   But man's natural bent for killing was hard to overcome and man crucified and killed the Devil's advocate.  This could have been the end of it, but the Devil is not so easily discouraged.  He appears to another man (maybe Paul) and convinces him to carry the message to the world.  Paul did a good job and for three hundred years or more his followers through passive resistance, which often lead to death, tried to spread the good news (gospels).  But, GOD was not to be defeated so easily.  He appears to Constantine for help.  Constantine adopts Paul's teaching as the national religion and converts it into a killing machine that rivals or exceeds that of any the other religions known to man.  The battles come and go but the war goes on.  The Devil sticks to his plan and currently, he seems to have the upper hand, for we surely seem to be dead set on exhausting our natural resources and destroying our environment, rendering it unfit for supporting many billions of people.  However, Christianity is only a minority religion and the battle may be going better elsewhere.  Take China for instance where a zero population growth is trying to be enforced.

We should not take any of this too seriously as far as our new GOD is concerned.  All that it might mean is that we won't need a Devil and there really is only one GOD.  However, there might be many angels, but we will learn only about the ones that spend their lives here on Earth.

It seems that little progress is being made toward developing a moral code and much of the progress that has been made appears to be counter productive.  But let's not give up.  Let's try to learn more about this new GOD and then return to this problem.  We may yet arrive at a moral code that is consistent with the teachings of our new GOD and comforting to man.

Where is GOD located and how does he control everything?  Where are his command centers and how does he control things from these centers?  For GOD some things never change, of course he is everywhere, but he is not homogeneous if he ever was.  He can be found in the innards of all the stars where fusion reactions produce the nucleus of heavy atoms.  In the center of, so called, Black Holes where we have yet to learn what goes on.  But more important, he is found in the nucleus of each atom.  Here GOD manifests (reveals) himself as the force that holds the protons and neutrons tightly together.  He is the energy that allows this to happen; that is, this energy is part of GOD.  GOD holds these nuclear particles together in a manner so that the positive electrostatic forces of the protons will attract electrons into specific energy levels until the combination is rendered neutral.  That is, an atom is formed.  The outer electrons (those further from the center) or valence electrons still exert short-range residual forces on those atoms that may be close by.  The nature of this residual short-range force determines what crystals are formed and what molecules are formed, etc.  You see GOD'S control center exists in the very small things, not the very large things.  GOD is both infinitely large and infinitely small.  But, it is the small that determines how the large will turn out.  Well now, is that all there is to it?  Is our GOD going to turn out to be just another nature GOD?  The answer to the first question is NO.  To the second the answer is, let's hope not, and let's not jump to final or semi-final conclusions so soon.

Let's try to look more closely at the "smallness" of GOD.  What holds the protons and the neutrons together?  What are they really made of?  I don't think that we really know; but, whatever it is, it is GOD too, and they are held together so that they strongly attract each other (even though they may possess electrical force they are very repulsive at these distances) and cause the atomic nucleuses to come together in just the proper way.  If we learn the answer to this question, it will raise other questions so that the quest for GOD continues, etc., etc., and etc.

Thus, whether we look for GOD in the small or in the large, we will keep passing him by as we continue our search.  Of course, I don't know, but I suspect that we will learn more and more about his control centers as we look smaller and smaller, and more and more about the results of the orders from these control centers as we look larger and larger.  Things on some large scale seem to repeat themselves.  Maybe we need to look no larger than our own galaxies or the collection of galaxies of which we are a part.  Do things also repeat at some point on a small scale?  Who knows?  Even if they did and we were to find something like a nuclear chromosome, we would still wonder how they came about.  Maybe we would have to start looking closer and closer at small things that exist only in the bowels of our largest and hottest stars.  Remember we are never going to know more than a finite amount, but let's keep looking and listening.  Maybe the Bible has it right where (in Hebrew 11.3) it says, *"That which is seen is made out of things which do not appear"*.

Before we return to the problem of our moral code, let's look more closely at what GOD has been and is telling us about biology of which we are a part. What does history tell us about biology?  History is the record of that which man thinks he knows about the past.  Therefore, history is but a fragment of biology and the life of man is but a small portion of the vicissitudes of organisms on land and in the sea.  Every living thing is a part of the food chain. It both consumes and is consumed, it eats and is eaten, and it competes for, takes and controls as much as possible.  All life is inextricably locked in a matrix so that they are in someway dependent upon each other and they compete for dominance.

Again the Lessons of History by the Durants provides valuable background information in Chapter III. Biology and History.  Their discussion is general, but the experiences of man are most often used for illustrations.  A copy of Chapter III is included here, but as before an attempt will be made to make the text coherent when this material is skipped.

# EXTRACT FROM
# LESSONS OF HISTORY

## Chapter III:  Biology and History

*By*
*Will and Ariel Durant*

In spite of several efforts to obtain permission to reproduce the copyrighted material in Chapters VII, VI and III of *The Lessons of History*, I have been unable to do so.

The following is a copy of the letter that was sent to the Will and Ariel Durant Foundation:

*"Dear Madam/Sir:*

*I have used three chapters from The Lessons of History in a work that I called "Rambling Thoughts on Raison d'entre (The Reason for Existing or the Meaning of it All)." I am not a professional author. I have written many scientific reports, papers, books and 70 patents. However, these works were not offered for sale. The above work is not a scholarly effort in that there are no footnotes and references are given only when I could remember them. There are no chapters and the work has not been edited in the sense that I have tried to not go back and change anything. I wanted to leave it just as the thought came to me.*

*Having been raised a Christian; I felt that the results of this work would only cause troubles with my Christian friends. Therefore, I wanted my wife to see if it was worth publishing only after I had passed on. Of course, an author generally thinks more of his work than anyone else would and it has been my experience that if the work is out of the field of his expertise or training, he is most likely suffering from an illusion.*

*Keeping these facts in mind, I would like to get an independent opinion and since most of my thoughts came from reading 'The Story of Civilization". I would value your opinion most of all – regardless of what that opinion may be.*

*As you will see, I have made an attempt to write so that the three chapters from "The Lessons of History" could be omitted, but for me, this would be a big loss.*

*I have also written an autobiography for my descendants, entitled "One of the Innumerable Stories that Generally remains Untold (Primarily for my Children and Grandchildren)." If you will allow me, I would like to send you a copy of these two works for your review. The biography is included so that you might understand the background of the author of "Rambling Thoughts" - that is seeing where I came from.*

*I apologize for the length of this message, but when I am asking for a lot, I felt an explanation was necessary. Your response is graciously requested."*

It is not reasonable to expect each reader to buy a copy of *The Lessons of History,* however, if you were to be exiled to an uninhabited tropical island and you could only take one book with you; then let that book be *"The Story of Civilization" by Will and Ariel Durant.*

# Resume Rambling Thoughts

COMPETITION is the first law of biology (one of GODS laws). Through this competition only the fittest will survive. In this manner the fittest are selected to carry on the fight. Selection is the second law of biology (another of GODS laws). The third law of biology is that life must breed (maybe this is the last of GODS laws of biology). These laws seem to be necessary and sufficient. Note that things including men are not created equal and they never will be. Nature loves differences as the necessary material of selection and evolution. Inequality is not only natural and in born, it grows with the complexity of civilization. Hereditary inequalities breed social and artificial inequalities, every invention or discovery is made or seized by the exceptional individual, and makes the strong stronger, and the weak relatively weaker. The best that one can hope for is an approximate equality of legal justice and educational opportunity.

Since these are GOD'S laws and since it is our lot to be the dominant predator, which must keep everything in balance for all times to come, let's recognize that this is so and accept our responsibility. Can we make a moral code that helps us accomplish this? Of course we can; but we don't want to sanction or encourage killing of men to accomplish it! Can we create a moral code that limits and maintains the world's human population levels without making killing moral? I don't know but let's try.

When we consider what needs to be done just in order to get started, we realize that the magnitude of the task is such that only GOD can do it and will do it with or without mans conscious help. His way without mans conscious help, will most likely be through starvation, or the introduction of new X-viruses to which man has no immunity. The new and unknown X-viruses may already exist in the depths of our rain forests and other remote locations. To avoid this let's try to consciously help GOD. I think that he would want us to, and has given us enough information for us to realize both the need to and maybe the way to accomplish it. What would we like to be done; what needs to be done; and what part of this can we start on now?

We would like for all people to realize the absolute necessity to conserve our natural resources and to use them sparingly. To always think of the future generations, all of them! To control birth to the point that the population can be maintained by our renewable resources and, most importantly, to realize that in doing so we are both obeying and giving thanks to GOD. The world is our church (the house of GOD) and taking care of it is both our duty to GOD and the rituals of our religion. It isn't that we are not interested in the rest of the universe; it's just that GOD has restricted our movement and possibly our influence to the near neighborhood of our solar system. Our duty to GOD is here and now.

Is not all of this going against GOD'S third law (all living things must breed)? Not really, all living things must breed, but only those living things, which are not their own worst predator need to breed as much as possible, that is as much as their predators will allow. Those that help control the ecology like the spider, humans, viruses, etc.; control their own population level. All but men do this by killing and consuming their own kind. Man from his beginning to the time of carbon fuels such as coal, oil and gas, performed his task in the same manner and to some extent is now attempting to do so. Consider Bosnia, the near east, Africa and other places.

Man has used the energy obtained from these fuels to create conditions that have bought the peoples of the world closer and closer together, and to develop methods for feeding increasingly larger numbers of people who require more and more of the available environment for their comfort. He has neglected his task of regulating his population level. These fuels exist in a finite amount. At the increasing rate that we are building a demand for them they will last for only a relatively short time and when they are gone, if we have not stabilized the human population, then to the sorrow of man, GODS will shall be done! Here GOD is more like the vengeful GOD of the Hebrews, (do as I say or pay the price) than like the loving GOD of the Trinity and Zoroaster.

Can we find other sources of energy that will allow us to continue developing and populating and "civilizing" the entire globe? Currently economic and population growth depends on what is called globalization. If we look to sources other than chemical and atomic like, wind, hydroelectric, solar, etc. we find that they are woefully inadequate. Can't atomic energy do the job? Perhaps fission fuels may be used, but they too are available in only finite amounts and can only increase the time we have to hear GOD and get on with his work. However, the problem of handling the fission waste created by the production of the required amount of energy, might severely limit the amount of time that can be gained. What about fusion energy where the waste problems are not so severe? It is true that the amount of fusion fuels available is staggering, but so far we only know how to produce this energy in an uncontrolled destructive manner, unless you want to consider underground explosions of fusion bombs controlled. Let's hope that man never resorts, even unintentionally, to the use of these weapons for population control.

It may seem far-fetched, but given enough time, man may learn to take advantage of natural phenomena like volcanic eruptions, title waves, hurricanes, tornadoes, earthquakes, ocean currents, global temperature difference, and the like, to capture store and then released this energy for future use. However, this may be even more difficult than solving the controlled nuclear fusion problem.

I have saved the geothermal sources so that they might be treated in a little more detail. The thermal energy stored and produced in the center of the earth is being used to help keep the earth's conditions stable. The magnitude of the energy stored and produced there is truly staggering. If we could only penetrate the Earth's material in a controlled (safe) manner, then we could force water down and get high temperatures, high-pressure steam in sufficient amounts to drive a very large complex of electrical generators. This energy could not only be distributed over a very large area, but it could also be used to produce fertilizer and other farm chemicals for shipment throughout the world. Hydrogen and oxygen could also be produced in large quantities for shipment. It might be possible to drive the indothermal reactions required to produce oil, gas, solvents and other lubricating liquids. It might be possible to create four or five of these complexes located so as to minimize the transportation requirements. This could solve our energy needs for a billion or more years.

Why have we not heard a lot about this before now? Some work has been done to penetrate the Earth's mantle that has failed. The job is not easy and you always have to be very careful when you might release the wrath of nature in a manner that you can't control. Also, the cost of attempting the above scheme would be very large, but so were the Manhattan Project and the project to put a man on the moon. Here we may need a project that is as large as or larger than both of these combined. The Manhattan Project and the NASA program keeps a lot of people employed, but like the pyramids in Egypt, they did not help to put food on the tables, clothes in the closets, or a roof over our heads and have not appreciably extended our energy resources. The above project could be the solution to this problem and therefore would justify the cost of bringing the best minds in the country to bear on this problem in a truly big way. The success of such an effort would not mean that we should not control the population levels. But now we could continue globalization and for a long time maintain a larger population at places where there would have otherwise not been enough energy to do so.

Why should man be different from the other dominant predators? Even though all things are part of GOD and GOD exist in all of them, only man is cognizant of GOD. Thus, for man GOD exists in the mind of man, which is GOD'S control center for man. The fear of GOD exists in his heart. It is through the mind that we sense GOD'S messages. It is through the mind that we must decide how to interpret and obey these messages. This is where free will comes in and only man has it. If GOD has given man a soul, this is it. Only man has a soul and it exist in his mind. Only man has been allowed to make a choice. All other living things must conquer and consume, and out reproduce, those things that conquer and consume them. Man, however, has been given the opportunity to control all things and to continue to do so if he can only learn to control himself. I think that GOD'S ultimate creation, at least here in our solar system, is the mind of man. We have been given the opportunity to be GOD'S "chosen" assistants. Let's seize this opportunity and try to evolve to the point that GOD can leave this task in our hands and not have to replace us with something else. However we must always remember that GOD is primarily interested in the species (in this case the human race) and not in the individual. Why is it this way? GOD'S control center of the race is in the chromosomes. It is through the chromosomes that man and all other life changes, evolves, and continues life. It is for this reason that the third law is that we must breed, and that GOD is concerned with the species and not the individual. Do all things that have a mind, have a soul? No, but they all have a spirit, and their mind is GOD'S control center for them. But except for man, they are not cognizant of GOD; do not have a soul or free will and the opportunity to choose to be one of GOD'S helpers. Their survival depends on their instincts alone. Do all living things even plants have a mind? I don't know. But, they have chromosomes and GOD sends us signals concerning this. Those who have spent their lives studying botany may already have the answer. Is there such a thing as a hereafter, a heaven or a hell? And if so have we been told anything about these things by GOD? All of this makes the formation of a comfortable moral code most difficult. But let's not give up yet.

We have seen that GOD speaks (sends the same signals) to all of us equally. But, there the equality ends. The ability to detect these signals, interpret them, explain them, and use the results to manipulate things, both animate and inanimate varies greatly from man to man. Most of this difference results from environmental, economic, and educational differences, some from heredity and such other things as birth defects.

Thus, it seems that GOD speaks to some better than to others, some who hear GOD best, such as our best scientists, develop understanding and physical laws that help produce devices that may be used to increase mans comforts or to destroy them and man himself. Free will not only comes in handy, but can also get in the way. This sword has two edges; it cuts both ways. Some others who hear GOD best use this information to either improve human conditions (on the average) or to make them worse. One of the best examples of this is Mahandas (called "Mahatma") Gandhi who attempted, without killing, to rid Africa and India of economic and authoritarian slavery. Some of the worst examples are Hitler, Stalin, Napoleon, Tojo, etc., etc., and etc.  Increasing freedom and improving economic conditions generally helps to reduce birth rates where wars, atrocities and natural disasters generally have the opposite effect.  Human technology has been used to enable man to support himself in ever increasing numbers.  But, this has been done at the cost of ever-increasing demands on our limited natural resources, and at the cost of ever increasing demands on our renewable resources.  There is also a price being paid as we contaminate our global environment more and more reducing its efficiency in supporting life.  Again these are the major things that man must change before his duty to GOD will be accomplished.  Then his duty will be easier, he will only have to perform the rituals of our worship.

If we are successful, what will the future be like?  Of course, I don't really know, but some things are clear.  First of all, rules will have to be developed that allows man to constrain his reproductive activities so that the population is maintained within the necessary limits.  It is hoped that man will be able to do this voluntarily out of respect for all future generations, out of a love of GOD, and as a demonstration of his devotion.  Secondly, energy will have to be used as efficiently as possible.  Travel for people will eventually be greatly reduced, and nearly all transportation will be by the cheapest possible method; thus, in mass transit to nearly everywhere.  Where will everywhere be?  That is, where are the people going to be?  They may be groups of population centers where everything that is needed for work, education, recreation, health care etc. are within distances that can be reached by walking or other forms of manual transportation, like bicycles or possibly by efficient electrically powered mass conveyances.  These population centers will be built in a matrix where they are connected by mass transit mainly for moving materials and necessary visitors for joint efforts and teams for local competitions, athletic and otherwise.  There may also be strategically placed centers where large sporting events, entertainment events, conventions, etc. may be presented.  The efficiency of the mass transit system to and from these centers will be maximized when strategically placed.  The space between these population centers may be used for controlled cultivation.  Even though, these areas may be reasonably large, transparent materials that can be used for a hothouse-effect may still cover them. These population centers are something like neighborhoods or small towns. The matrix is something like a city. There will be many such cities throughout the world and all cities will be ultimately connected by electronics, mostly wireless, so that personal contact is available to all at anytime. It may be best if population is controlled at the small town or the city level. This does not mean that all towns and cities will be of the same size. Size may depend on the resources and the conditions at each locale. Each locale should be as self-sufficient as is reasonable so that the need to distribute things on a large scale is minimized. Of course, there will still be some specialization. Some places will be able to produce many copies of some things that cannot be efficiently produced at other places and the distribution of these things will be necessary. But no one should import more than is really necessary.

The much larger areas between the cities will contain really large agricultural area for planting and grazing and the large ecological areas that may be called world parks or global parks. Much of the available energy resources will have to be devoted to working and maintaining these areas so that they are mechanized and not labor intensive.

But, what about racial problems? Do they just go away? Isn't this all just another Utopian dream? How is it to be governed? People will still be people; who is going to settle their differences? Will greed and the injustices it causes just disappear? We can discuss all these questions, but it will take time. However, the above vision of the future is intended to be a utopia only in the way the available energy supply is to be expended, and population is to be controlled. These two things are the way we recognize and give thanks to GOD. Of course, actual solutions may be quite different from the above city-state concept. The outcome will depend upon the development of so-called alternate energy sources and the evolution of engineering and agricultural technologies. The answer to the last questions is an unfortunate NO! But maybe we can find a way to minimize even the undesirable effects of basic instincts; let's try.

Man seems to have recognized that, through the cognizance of GOD, he has been able to learn part of GOD'S rules (The Laws of Nature) and how to use them to manipulate the environment and to control it to a great extent.

But, he has not yet realized that he must use this knowledge to control himself in a manner that benefits all future generations.

GOD has written the promise of the resurrection in the birth of every offspring, plant or animal. Man has written his version of this promise in books, and in most of them he has only included himself. Why is man's version so different from GOD'S? First of all, man thinks that only he is made in the image of GOD (man's own doing) and only he is qualified to be with GOD forever more. He doesn't fully realize that he is with and is part of GOD at all times. Secondly, man thinks that he knows it all; how things will end, when they will end, who will be "saved", and who won't. Clearly man "knows" too much for his own good and has no real concept of what infinity really means. But this has not always been the case. For example, in the Old Testament one of the Prophets, when asked, "Why must good people suffer?" answered: "to serve all future ages as well as the dismal present. The purpose of the infinite GOD cannot be understood by the finite mind of man. But GOD'S justice, mercy and righteousness are unchangeable and everlasting." This question is also addressed in the Book of Job, which contains many lessons, but the greatest of these lessons comes from GOD when he warns all mankind that we cannot hope to understand His ultimate purpose – the divine will. Job answers for all of us when with trust and goodness he says, "Though he slays me, yet I will trust him…" "Behold the fear of the Lord, that is wisdom and to depart from evil is understanding…." The old prophet was right, we cannot comprehend GOD'S ultimate purpose, but we can understand that to achieve that purpose GOD is primarily interested in the species and not the individual.

Let's try again to look for a moral code. People cannot govern themselves without a leader. Some one or something must organize, direct and control. To do this they must have authority and power to go along with responsibility. But, men are men and men are corrupted by power. Thus, no government by one man or a few men will meet our needs for long. We must look to a government run by the Rule of Law and the law must apply to all, even the chief administrator in so far as his violations of the law are for personal gain and for the good of not all. Realizing, of course, that the good of all does not always translate into the good of each individual and that sometimes the righteous and unrighteous are affected alike even by acts of the government.

There are two primary purposes of the government.  The first is to see that in so far as is possible, everyone is fed and clothed, and that equal legal and educational opportunities are made available to all.  Recreation and health care will also be made available as equally as circumstances permit.  The primary aims of the educational systems will be to train people so that they can better our ability to increase the efficiency of the utilization of our natural and renewable resources.  The second primary purpose is to control the population level.  This level is not necessarily some fixed number.  It will vary from place to place and at any place from time to time.  It will depend on the resources available and their projected availability.  The birth rate would need to be adjusted from time to time to take into account the forecasted resource levels.  The population levels will be maintained where some safety factor is taken into account.  Killing will not be resorted to unless our moral code, when it is developed, allows for it, in some cases, like those that may prevent suffering; or in extreme cases where the preservation of the species depends on it.

To achieve these two primary purposes, by peaceful means, the government will need to be global and our moral code will need to solicit and if necessary demand the cooperation of each individual.  What shall this moral code contain?  It will contain rules (commandments) that reward virtues and condemn sins.  What is a virtue and what is sin?  A virtue will be any quality or behavior that promotes people to get along with each other and in so far as possible, to love and respect each other.  These qualities will also help people to love and respect GOD and to voluntarily obey and help the government achieve its purpose.  A sin is any quality or property that tends to prevent people from getting along peacefully and in harmony. That is, it is the opposite of a virtue.  For example, to love GOD and to want to help the government peacefully maintain the proper population level would be the chief or highest virtue.  To waste or through gluttony, use up our natural resources would be the chief or highest sin.  Thus, you can see that most of the developed countries are now living in sin and our efforts at globalization where all countries are to be developed only increases that sin.  This does not mean that we should stop helping other countries to develop.  It means that we should begin our efforts to make the developed countries much more conservative and efficient and to bring the population growth to a halt until we can figure out what population levels are proper.

What then are GOD'S commandments?  First, let's consider the virtues for they are the "thou shalls":

1. Thou shall love GOD and always consider the welfare of all future generations.
2. Thou shall love, respect, and cooperate with your neighbors to achieve GODS ends.
3. Thou shall love, honor, and train your children in the ways of righteousness.
4. Thou shall love and honor your father and mother and be thankful for their training.
5. Thou shall observe at least one day of rest each week in honor of GOD.

Now let us consider sins for they shall be the "thou shall nots":

6. Thou shall <u>NOT</u> commit murder.
7. Thou shall NOT steal.
8. Thou shall NOT lie.
9. Thou shall NOT commit adultery.
10. Thou shall NOT have more than one mate at a time.
11. Thou shall NOT commit incest
12. Thou shall NOT father or give birth to more than two children, except in the case of multiple births and unless your children precede you before they have children or in cases where it is desirable to restore the population level.
13. Thou shall NOT be envious or covet that which belongs to another, but it is alright to admire.
14. Thou shall NOT be jealous for it hurts all that are involved, especially you.

Well, now we have 14 commandments instead of the 10 that we are accustomed to.  We have also left out worship no other GODS but me, worship no idols or images, and don't take the LORD'S name in vain.  The worship of other GODS that does not require violations of the above commandments is not condemned.  Gods to whom human sacrifices are made like the God of Transportation and the God of Dangerous Sports are permitted.  Gods like Dioceses; the God of wine and rivalry might be tolerated if their followers don't interfere with the rights of others.  Some idols or images may be permitted.  For example, sports idols, great leaders, and all of nature, as we know it can be taken as an image of GOD.  Also, certain scientific laws as we know them and as they evolve can be taken as GOD'S words or as images of a part of GOD.  As for remembering the Sabbath and keeping it holy, it should be realized that this is an arbitrary thing that was made for man by man and not by God.  This is just one of the many places where The Bible is in error.  God did not complete creation, cease and then rest forever.  God did not, has not, and is not resting.  God never has and it seems that he never will rest.  It seems that the Jews kept what they called the seventh day sacred.  This day came to be called Saturday.  As a child, I was taught that Christ being a Jew also kept this day holy and did not rise from the dead until the next day – Sunday and at the time this to me seemed logical.  But it did not explain why nearly the entire Christian world now keeps Sunday, at least to some extent, holy.   This happened because Constantine, who was an excellent killer, emperor of the Roman Empire and defacto, Head of the Christian Church, but not yet a Christian, decided to change the holy day to Sunday because upon that day Christ was supposed to have risen from the dead.  He liked Sunday better than some day that tied the Christian Religion strongly to Jehovah.  This helps the Christian Church somewhat separate itself from Judaism and more independently represented only the Gentiles. After the dispersion of the Jews and the rise of Christianity, there was for centuries in the cradle of religions, a large area where a great number of people lived that were not members of one of the major world religions.  They were neither Egyptians, Jews, Christians, Hindu nor Buddhist.  This void was filled in an explosive manner when Mohammed brought forth a new religion by changing Jehovah into Allah and to create Islam.  Similar to Constantine, he wanted to be independent from both the Jews and the Christians, so he created a new calendar and made Friday the Holy Day.

The bottom line is that in each religion the days that are set aside as holy or otherwise days of rest are arbitrary. Thus, for our religion the choice of these days are to be made by the government and they may vary from place to place and from time to time, as best benefits the people and their customs. Remember it is the spirit of worship that is important not its form. What you want to do is to be just, to love mercy and to walk humbly with your GOD. Occasionally, you should do what only holy men seem to do. That is, to go off to yourself, in silence and solitude, try to listen to GOD, reflect on what you hear and pray for understanding.

Note that we have not included anything about homosexuality, fornication, masturbation, prostitution and abortion. It turns out that there is no inherent sin in homosexuality! And, there is no sin inherent in the act of fornication as long as it is with another unmarried consenting adult person. However, both may lead to complications that tend to cause sins to be committed. Other laws can and should be passed that deal with these cases. Masturbation is not sinful. It may be helpful when it relieves pressure. But, it could lead to other sins being committed, in cases where one fails to recognize the difference between fantasy and reality. Other laws will again deal with the results. What about prostitution? It does not seem that prostitution is necessarily sinful, except when one or more of the partners are married. When masturbation is not adequate, prostitution may have beneficial results. In most cases it is just the culmination of a business contract for fornication, and any sinful results should be treated as such. However, for the prostitute, and consequently for the customer, the necessity of frequently changing partners can make this profession more dangerous than profitable. What about abortion? This is a tough one. Are they in and of themselves a sin? No, not when they are performed for the purpose of insuring the longevity of our natural resources and our species. They should be treated in some sense like that of multiple births. There will always be some people who do not for one reason or another have children or father children. If there were no allowance made for extra births, then the population would tend to decline. Multiple births alone would not be enough to stabilize the population level. Unwanted or illegal pregnancies could be used to bring the birth rate back to the desired level. However, the offenders would have to be chastised in some way and generally this should be sufficient, but if they are repeat offenders, they would need to be sterilized. They could be sterilized after the first offense if the birth rate at that time warrants it.

Aren't GOD'S justice, mercy and righteousness constant in time and space, unchangeable and everlasting? Well we have seen that virtues and therefore sins seem to change from time to time and from place to place. Obviously, there was a time when it was beneficial for man to reproduce as much as possible in order to survive. Well then, is the answer NO? I don't think so. For nearly all of Man's existence, that is, for the first few hundred thousands or few million years, whatever the case may be, man's message from GOD as he interpreted it, was to survive, expand, multiply, push back the wilderness and learn to efficiently use the renewable resources. He also was cognizant of GOD in many confused ways, but he somehow knew that he was to be the most dominant species. During this time he learned to make use of some of the natural resources such as stones, metals, wood, water, etc. for building homes, tools, defenses and weapons which were used for both hunting and for war, killing that is. When resources were scarce in one region and more plentiful in another, war was eminent. Rather than share, they would fight until enough were killed for the available resources to be more than sufficient. To the victor, goes the spoil. However, this does not mean that the population level of the world went down or even remain the same. Elsewhere, new lands were being cleared and new communities were being developed and growing until they too had enough surpluses to require defending. Also tremendous technological advances were being made. Among these were learning how to build, control and use fire for several different purposes; acquiring the ability to domesticate animals for food, clothing, tools, etc.; and the ability to properly harness animals for labor such as plowing and transportation. But, what about thou shall not kill? In some of my copies of The Bible, it is written thou shall not kill, but in other editions it is written thou shall not commit murder. Things always seem to change; words themselves move about and change their very meaning. We chose to use the word murder instead of kill in our commandments, so that we could have them mean different things, for, as we shall see there will always be a need to kill. It would have been better had all the translations of the Bible done the same. Obviously killing was moral when the Hebrew GOD told his people to make war on another group of people and to kill every man, woman and child, in order to obtain their land and other valuables.  Also, in the case where GOD killed the first-born child of every Egyptian, killing couldn't have been against GOD'S laws and therefore was not immoral!  However, for one Hebrew, to kill another would be murder and would be immoral.  It may have been better for the Hebrews to do as they thought they heard GOD say.  They for the most part did not and sure enough, these people came back to "haunt" them and are doing so even today.

Under our moral code similar, not immoral, killings could take place.  For example, when people are old, feeble, suffering, and are no longer able to enjoy life or contribute to the well being of others, they may (for their own sake and for the sake of those soon to be born) be killed. There are other types of killings that are necessary and obviously not immoral.  More about this later.

Let's not forget that before the era of great scientific advances in all fields which overlap the era of carbon fuels, in which we now exist, man was and still is in the expansion stage.  He was not cognizant of a need to conserve natural resources.  He seemed to regard them as sufficient to last forever.  Even today, most people seem to think that way and nearly all of us act as if it were so.  These fuels are being used primarily to produce chemicals that make our lands capable of producing foodstuffs to feed many billions of people (yet, some live in poverty and don't even have enough to eat), and increase transportation to the point where tourism is a world-wide industry, affordable by many; and to drive massive construction and manufacturing industries that have made unheard of comforts and luxuries available to more people in the developed countries, and to the leaders of the developing and underdeveloped countries.

How long do we have before we must do something about getting this religion started?  When will it be too late to prevent man due to his selfishness, gluttony, greed and the lack of understanding from condemning all future generation to lives of chaos and suffering?  If we don't see the light soon, it may be too late.  But what should we do first?  First let's try to insure that there will always be plenty of good food, clean water, and efficient use of energy.  What should the world's diet be?  Let's consider two cases, a plant-based (vegetarian) diet and a meat-centered diet.

If plant-based diets were to be aggressively promoted and adopted by (just) the American public, the need for expensive and potentially hazardous energy sources would be greatly reduced. This means cutting out or nearly cutting out the consumption of meat, especially beef and pork. According to the Departments of Interior and Commerce, the value of raw materials consumed to produce food from livestock is greater than the value of all oil, gas and coal consumed in this country. Not only is a tremendous amount of energy consumed by the meat industry, but also half of all the water consumed in the United States is needed. In addition to the water used to irrigate land for the growing of feed for livestock, the monstrous livestock factories that have replaced traditional forms to wash away the animal's excrement, etc. use great quantities of water. According to News Week, "the water that goes into a 1,000 pound steer is enough to float a destroyer." The energy used to bring food to the animals and for climate control at these factories is enormous. The bottom line is that the energy cost of producing plant foods is approximately ten times less than that for raising animal flesh. By switching to a primarily vegetarian diet, plus limits on export of non-essential fatty foods, enough money would be saved to cut our imported oil requirements by more than 60 percent. Also, the supply of renewable energy sources such as wood and hydroelectric could be increased by as much as 150 percent.

On the other hand, if all humans were to eat a meat-centered diet, the world's petroleum reserves would last about 13 years. However, if everyone ate a vegetable diet these reserves would last for 200 years. If we take into account technological advances that might allow for the use of coal reserves as a replacement for oil, then we may be good for 200 year even with meat to eat, and quite a bit longer with a plant-based diet. But even this case does not allow for population expansion and two or three centuries are an extremely short time when one is concerned about all future generation! If we could stop the world's population growth, reverse it, and reduce the population by, say, 25% and hold it at that level, then we would have a great deal of time to work with. Maybe even enough to convince the world of the need to prepare for times many milleniums ahead. [For references see Energy & Vegetarianism by Carla Bennett in the June 6, 2001 issue of the Huntsville Times.]

To better grasp how fast the increase in the rate, at which our natural resources are being exhausted, let's consider just the case of oil and transportation. This may be illustrated by the following sequence of events. In 1769 horses were introduced to the Indians in California – use of oil none.  In 1869 this country was spanned by a railroad when the Golden Spike was driven in Promontory Point, Utah – USE OF OIL NEARLY NONE.  At this time trains use steam power, which was produced, by the use of wood and coal.  In 1900 there were about 8,000 automobiles in our hemisphere, essentially all in the United States.  But there were only 10 miles of paved roads – USE OF OIL VERY LITTLE.  When the 1930's began there were only a few hundred thousand cars in the United States.  When the 1930's ended there were more than twenty-six million - USE OF OIL -CONSIDERABLE.  In 1903 the era of aviation began when the Wright Brothers made a flight of 120 yards (including the take off and landing) – USE OF OIL – very little.  In 1969 man was landed on the moon – USE OF OIL just to develop, test, and perfect the rockets – CONSIDERABLE. Today consider not what percent of the families have cars, but how many cars we have per family; how many vehicles are used by industry and businesses and what percent of the families own airplanes (yes airplanes, in Alaska this is 25%).  Consider the size of the military air power and the commercial airlines where UPS is the largest airline in the world.  When you are driving down the road, look at the cars you see and, yes, the airplanes you see or hear; and think of each of these as a small leak in the natural containers that hold our oil reserves.  Think also of the roads and the maintenance they require as additional leaks.  Then remember that through globalization, we are trying to make the whole world look like this.  Then try to realize that the chemical industry requires more oil than transportation and that this may also be the case for the electrical power industry.  Although there are many other uses of oil, the above should give you a good idea of how we are rapidly going to hell on an oil slick instead of in a hand basket.

We are not only using up our natural resources, but we are also destroying our renewable resources, at an equally alarming rate.  For example, the long-leaf pine forests were once one of the greatest forests on Earth, covering approximately ninth-two million acres from Virginia to Texas.  Today, less than thirty percent of this forest remains and what is left is disappearing at the rate of one hundred thousand acres per year.  At this rate, they will last less than three hundred years.  This may seem like a long time, but in a few hundred years carbon fuels will become scarce and this rate will go up.  Unless the current trend is stopped and reversed, the once magnificent long leaf pine forest will disappear.  This was not what GOD intended.  Man has failed and is failing to make the right choices in this case.  This forest presents a case where killing is good and man could take advantage of this fact if he does it right.  For most forest fire is the enemy, but it is as important to long leaf pine forest as rain is to the tropical forest.  Take away fire and long-leaf forest would cease to exist.  You see if man would just leave these forests alone, then GOD will take care of them through nature with rain and fire.  If we need to kill these trees for our needs and comforts then we must try to replace the ones we use or take them in a pattern that helps accomplish what fires do.  This may include using controlled burns when needed.  (An article appeared in The Huntsville Times - date unknown – that discussed in detail the history of the long-leaf pine forest.  I saved this article, but I cannot locate it and therefore cannot properly reference it.)

This may be a good place to express a few thoughts about "global warming".  The temperature of the Earth has varied throughout time.  There have been several cycles where there was "global cooling" and ice accumulated from the poles toward the equator.  These were called ice ages.  These were followed by periods of "global warming" where the ice melted and the area where the ice remained solid moved back toward the poles.  None of these periods had anything to do with what man was doing or was capable of doing.  We will call these phenomena long-term natural variations.  During any one of these periods the increase or decrease of the mass of the ice layers was not monotonic.  That is there were also short-term natural variations and none of these had anything to do with mans activities here on Earth.  They were caused primarily by relatively small percentage changes or fluctuation in the surface temperature of the sun, (the energy radiated by the sun varies as the forth power of the temperature) and possibly by earth events, like very large volcano eruptions, periods of high volcanic active or very extensive forest fires.  However, most of this occurred before the advent of the recorded history of civilization.  During the current period we have been in a "global warming" phase.  There have been some short-term variations during this phase, but up until the last fifty or so years they have all been due to natural variables and not due in any real extent to man's behavior.  Remember the temperatures that we are concerned with are surface air temperatures and the subsurface ocean temperatures. They are statistical numbers, mean or averaged numbers, and cannot be used to explain singular events. For example the recorded high temperatures for a region in Alaska (Nome, I think) was well over 100 degrees F and this was near or before 1900 AD, while the record low was recorded very recently. This does not mean that we are not in a period of global warming, even for the short-term. We really are in a period of global warming. This should not be denied. However, we should go slowly when it comes to stating causes or placing blame. Some people always think that man is more capable than he really is, especially when it comes to doing damage. Right now humans are responsible for about 7.8 billion tons of greenhouse gases produced annually. This is a tremendous amount, but it is just 4.5% of the 173.1 billion tons produced annually, mostly by volcanic eruptions, seawater evaporation and decaying matter. You see humans are not responsible for the problem; they can only make the problem a little worse.

A United Nations Panel has warned of global temperatures rising by 10.5 degrees over the next one hundred years in a worse case scenario. In this case, melting Antarctic ice could raise sea levels by up to ten feet over the next one thousand years. Well now, this seems to be at most a second-order problem. We are already worrying about running out of carbon fuels in a few hundred years, at which time our ability to adversely affect the "global warning" problem will be greatly reduced. Never the less, we should solve these problems as the opportunities present themselves. But, at all times, we should keep our first-order problems in mind while working on the second-order problems and not do anything that makes the first-order problems worse.

We are changing subjects to discuss reincarnation. What about reincarnation? Does it really happen? If so, how can we tell? What about the case of the Dahli Lama? Does he return again and again to show his people the way to life everlasting? I think that the answer to most of these questions is yes. But if the answers are yes, then how does reincarnation occur, and why does it occur. First it occurs because GOD'S primary concern is the preservation of the species and he accomplishes this by reproduction of the individuals, at least in part. If we start with one of the more simple cases, that of plants and flowers, it seems that daisies reproduce to produce daisies just like or nearly like themselves. That is they are reincarnated! Through mutations or cross breeding some variations can be produced, but, in general, these variations can reincarnate themselves. Thus, we see that reincarnation occurs through and according to GOD'S instructions that are contained in the chromosomes. Of course, the reason it occurs is to preserve the species. The above applies to all of the known plants.

For what seems to be more complicated cases, like insects, the above conclusions also apply. Species like, spiders and all other animal species except man are not only more complicated but seem to be progressively more complicated. This seems to be the case because GOD'S control center for each of these animals is in the brain. Thus it is separated from the chromosomes. The animals are mobile and seek their own mates rather than needing an external agent for pollination. One of the most beautiful and easily observed examples of this is a butterfly, where metamorphosis can be observed. These animals have a spirit. The spirit of most animals, differ greatly from one species to another. This spirit resides in the brain and it is what differentiates the animals from plants.

Man was excluded from the above discussion because man not only has a brain and a spirit, but he also has a soul. Man alone is cognizant of GOD! This cognizance comes through his soul. But as we have seen, this cognizance of GOD does not mean that man will automatically recognize GOD'S will. This makes man the most complicated of all species. He is to control the population of all things including mankind and is free to choose how to do it. The preceding chapters have indicated how our new religion thinks this should be done.

Back to reincarnation. Is man reincarnated? Yes, but only in part. Mankind receives one chromosome from his father and one from his mother. (This does not include the case of parthenogenesis, where virgin birth insures the reincarnation of part the mother except possibly for her soul.) Consequently, the child is a reincarnation of part of both of his parents. If the child is a male, then he has received one of his chromosomes, the "Y" chromosome from his father, who received it from his father, who received it from his father, etc., etc., etc. So, this child is a reincarnation, at least in part, of his biological male line. What about the other chromosome, the "X" chromosome? He received this from his mother. Therefore reincarnation, at least in part, is of his mother. But which of her two "X" chromosomes did he receive? His mother had one from her father and one from her mother. In the first case, he is a re-incarnation, at lease in part, of his mother's father; who was a reincarnation, at least in part, of her mother; who was a reincarnation, at lease in part, of either her father or her mother, who.. etc., etc., etc. Similar (and hopefully not confusing) statements can be made for the case where the "X" chromosome came from his grandmother. In the case when the child is a girl, we have to go through the same kind of considerations for both "X" chromosomes. Is all this really reincarnation, even in part? Yes it is, because, no matter how devious the path, your chromosomes have come down to you from distant in-dividuals, and except for possibly accidental mutations, they are just like the chromosomes of your ancestors. You were reincarnated (born or born again) according to GOD'S exact instructions, as were your ancestors.

Does this mean that the soul is also reincarnated? Maybe and maybe not! If you have a soul, is your soul the same as that of one of your ances-tors? Are souls reused? Do souls really differ one from another? If not then most of these questions may be irrelevant. If at birth, one soul is not different from another, then what difference does it make? Our souls give each of us a chance to make a choice how we will interpret and do GOD'S will. When we die our individual bodies are of no more use to GOD in so far as helping or not helping to accomplish his will is concerned. Like the animals, our spirits die with our bodies, but what about our souls? Do they also just die? I don't think so. It is not as if they were material things or that they never existed. The nature of the future of mankind is determined by the choices they made. Our souls came from GOD and they remain with GOD. Of course, he may reuse them or not reuse them as he sees fit. Maybe he reuses the ones that did not make the "right" choices, so that they may be punished by having to endure the havoc that they caused. In any case this is one of the things that GOD was talking about when he told Job that the finite mind of man is not capable of comprehending the infinite. It might be that the people of Tibet and the Dhala Lama have it right. They certainly conserve their natural resources and live off their renewable resources. Let's hope that they are allowed to re-turn to their country. It may be that the world will need to study their ways as an example of doing things right including being peaceful and loving one another.

Is this all that one would like to know about reincarnation? Of course not, there are many more questions. Some examples are: Does everyone have a soul? Did prehistoric man have a soul? Does mankind have a soul today? Do newborn babies have a soul before, or at birth? If not when do they get one? Does everybody get one? If you do get one, can you lose it? If you once lose it can you get it back? Are all souls the same; that is, do they really differ one from another, even at the start? So many questions – so few answers. Most if not all of this falls under the category of things that the finite mind does not yet fully understand. But let's not use this as a cop out. Let's see where our reason or logic takes us. For a long time prehistoric men differed little from other animals, he survived and multiplied by instinct alone. Natural resources like hydrocarbon fuels were unknown and renewable resources in most cases seemed inexhaustible and had to be destroyed in order to make room for man and to supply his comforts. Early on, he had no real comprehension of one GOD as the creator of everything. At this time, it seems that men did not have a soul. Later on he developed a sense of the supernatural and many GOD'S were created to address one fear or another. In different places and at different times, man became cognizant of GOD, the creator. At these times and in these places man acquired (was granted by GOD) a soul. He was now able to receive and start to interpret the signals that GOD was and is sending to help him exercise his free will for the good of all including, all those who are yet to come. Remember that GOD'S plan is to preserve the human species, and for man to help him do so. How man needs to do this is a function of time. At first it was most important for man to increase his kind and learn to cooperate with each other so that he was strong enough and widespread enough and smart enough to control everything but himself. There was plenty for everybody but life was much easier in some places that in others and this led to conflicts, wherein man began to try to control his population density. He also tried to control his density by expansion through migration. All of them worked for many eons except in isolated places like the Polynesian Islands where people built stone "GODS" and failed to preserve their renewable resources (trees) until these islands could no longer support life and the human population passed away. It seems that they had a free will, but they made the wrong choices. Of course, we must prevent this from happening on a much larger scale. If these people had a soul, then it looks like they lost them and at least they will not get them back.

Does all mankind have a soul today? In the sense that having a soul means being cognizant of GOD and having a free will, the answer is obviously no. Unborn children and newly born children don't seem to have a soul. How could they be cognizant of GOD? These children will acquire (be granted by GOD) a soul when their parents, or their society train them to the point where they have learned enough about GOD to be able to receive him (become cognizant of GOD). What if these children grow up and don't receive a soul? Does that mean that their descendants will not have a soul? No it does not, these descendants will also in their time have a chance to acquire a soul and how they use it will depend primarily on their education and their society rather than on who their ancestors were.

Of course, all of these things that have been said about the soul are speculation based on our guesses about what the soul is and what seems, to us, to be GOD'S will. It may well be that the soul evolved with man and it is still evolving. It may be that some souls are punished after a person is dead and that some are rewarded, but we have no way of knowing where or how. So, for now, all we can do is listen to GOD, try to understand what we are being told, prepare for the future here on earth, and hope for the best. Our ability to reason about the hereafter as far as the soul is concerned has come, at least temporarily, to an end; and to proceed we must depend on faith alone. When our beliefs are based on faith alone, anything is possible. We can believe, like some of the early Egyptians that there are eleven heavens and seven hells! We can believe like Zoroastrians and Christians that there is only one heaven and one hell and then like some of the Christians, we can believe that some in hell are punished more than others and that some in heaven are rewarded (or loved) more than others. To do this we must compartmentalize heaven and hell then it seems to me that we are nearly back to where the early Egyptians were. On faith alone, it is all right to have believes like Marshall Applewhite and the Heaven's Gate Cult did in California in 1997 and go to heaven as a group on the Hale-Bopp Comet. I think it is best to forget about heaven and hell and to just trust GOD and to let him take care of our souls in whatever way he things is an appropriate manner.  Let's adopt the epitaph at the grave of the Indian Chief Kankapod:

> *"O GOD here lies Chief Kankapod,*
> *Treat his soul gently O GOD,*
> *Treat it as if he were GOD,*
> *And you were Chief Kankapod."*

So far we have not found a need for hell, but if we do there are two things that we can be sure of.  First, either we have a free will or there is no hell.  If there is no free will then everyone does God's will and this is the one thing for which no one will be punished.  Second, if there is a free will, then a hell is possible, but if there is a hell there will be no eternal punishment, for no finite sin or amount of sins will justify eternal punishment. The Golden Rule might be easier for one to follow if it is thought of in its negative connotation - "Don't do unto others, as you don't want them to do unto you".  Some examples are.  If you don't want someone to steal from you, then don't steal from anyone.  If you don't want someone to murder you, then don't murder anyone.  If you don't want someone to commit adultery with your mate, then don't commit adultery with anyone.  If you don't want someone to vandalize or trash your property, then don't vandalize or trash anyone else's property; and so forth and so on, etc.

This is something analogous to the 10 commandments.  You have your positive commands – the I shall – and your negative commands – the I shall nots.  It seems to me that most of the time it is easier to know what not to do.

Let's get back to killing, for we must know when to kill and when not to kill.  Who really believes that it would have been immoral for Noah to kill those two mosquitoes and fleas?  In general killing is neither bad nor immoral and it is necessary when survival depends upon it. Also, poison is necessary for the life of the serpents and the spiders, but it carries death for others.  Here both killing and being killed are part of God's will and is not immoral.  Man is the dominant predator of all things.  Predators kill; therefore it is necessary for man to kill.  Let's divide things that may need to kill or be killed into classes or groups.  The word SENTIENT means, being responsive, having a consciousness of sense and impressions, being aware, capable of sentiment, having emotions, understanding emotional idealism. All of which requires a brain. The word non-sentient means without feeling as the sentient understands it. This group includes all vegetation and all other organisms like bacteria, viruses, etc., that we assume can not feel pleasure or pain. I think that these two groups include all of the living organisms, however the demarcation lines that separate them may be, let's say, fuzzy.

Let's first consider the non-sentient group. Are the members of this group, killers? You can bet they are; all of them are killers. The softwood trees grow fast and kill the shade intolerant grasses and most of the underbrush. Prepare your lawn with a special grass and don't protect it from native grasses and see what happens. The hardwood trees grow slower but they eventually shade the softwood trees and kill them off to produce a mature forest. All vegetation does "battle" with each other, first to survive and then to expand and dominate. Current conditions will determine who is winning and changing conditions will determine who is winning at a later time. This is just their way of participating in the battle for survival of the fittest, which means those most capable of adapting, will be the survivors. Also let's not forget that some plants (poison ones) can kill animals and some even catch and eat such things as flies. None of this killing is bad.

As for the sentient group it needs to be divided into two subgroups. The first group will contain all of the animals except humans. The second group will consist of the humans. The first subgroup needs to be further divided into two classes – the Carnivorous (meat eaters) and the herbivorous (plant eaters). The herbivorous kill the members of the non-sentient group but only when they need food. This is not bad; it is good. These animals are the predators that help control the populations of the plants for God. They are doing God's will. The other class, the carnivorous, kill the herbivorous animals, but, again they only kill in order to eat which helps to control the population of the plant eaters, which is again according to God's will. This class, the meat-eating animals also tend to kill each other. Sometimes they kill for the control of the food supply, sometimes in self-defense, and sometimes they also kill and eat each other. Consider the reptiles for example. This helps to thin their population. We must remember that before the time of man, this class was their number one predator and when easy prey was not plentiful they went after each other.  Here they played the part that the spiders play for the insects.

The last class, the humans are the best killers of all.  Even though they could not survive in a "fair" fight with some of the other animals, they are still the best killers for several reasons.  First they learned to fight like dogs in packs.  At this time they primarily killed the herbivorous sub-group for food and the carnivorous sub-groups in self-defense and for dominance of the food supply.  None of this killing is bad.  Later, they improved their verbal communication skills; their weapons, their organizing abilities, and their packs became armies of sorts.  Now they would do battle and kill each other until the spoils – women, children, weapons, valuables, hunting territories, planting areas (that is cleared land) and etc. were the properties of the winners.  Were these killing bad?  This may seem to be a hard question, but, I think the answer was and maybe still is no!  Life on the planet earth may have continued in this manner (forever and ever "nearly") where man determines how many of each group including his own that the renewable resources of the earth will sustain at any time.  In this case man was and still is supposed to do what no other animals can do – that is to plan ahead for their future.  Other animals plan ahead, but for only one year.  Squirrels hide food for the winter; bears store fat, etc.  But only man can plan ahead for years, decades, centuries, millenniums and eons to come.

What is it about man that makes him really different from the other organisms?  It is his ability to communicate verbally, to communicate in writing, to communicate electronically, to organize, to cooperate, etc.  In short, it is his ability to reason and be able to learn.  Only man has this ability and since only man has a soul, this must be part of his soul.  It is the part of the soul through which GOD communicates with man.  Thus, it is through reason that man must learn GOD'S plan and try to understand man's part in this plan.  Man must do this if our planet is to be a safe haven for his life in the future.  Anything that we want to believe about GOD'S plan beyond this must be based on faith.  When ones belief is based on faith he is professing to "know" too much.  This is neither in, nor of itself, bad or good.  It is bad when it hinders the carrying out of GOD'S plan, as determined by GOD'S communications with us through reason (through the soul).  It is good when it encourages the development of this plan.  Accepting the teachings of men like Jesus, Gandhi, Buddha, etc. on faith could be good, but blindly following the religions that have evolved from them and have been contaminated by other men has and could lead to bad killings.

I believe that nearly everyone who reasons knows that it is alright to kill the ants that invade your yard, to kill the pest that damage your crops or contaminate your water, to kill a wild animal in self defense, to kill the weeds that invade your garden, and a thousand other cases. However, there are some that believe that we should not kill endangered species. Nothing should be allowed to become extinct. For example, if the only habitat for the snail darter would be destroyed if we build a dam, that would help to control our water supply and to irrigate land for increasing our renewable resources and to produce power that might be used to make fertilizer for the same purpose, then it should be (so long it has been nice to know you, but I have got to be moving along) bye, bye snail darters. It must be realized that becoming extinct always has been and still is part of GOD'S plan. This discussion could go on and on, but before we leave killing for a while, let's try to see when killing is bad and when it is really bad. Any killing that is unnecessary (whatever that may be) is bad. Any killing that is wasteful of our renewable resources is bad. Any killing of things in the first two groups where we use those things that are killed for our needs or comforts and don't make efforts to help the species to renew itself are to some extent also bad. When we carry this kind of killing to the extent that we threaten the existence or even the necessary abundance of these needed renewable resources then it is really bad. When we kill one another for personal gain, dislike or revenge (murder) it is bad. When we do this on a large scale, especially against one group or race, it is really bad. When will we learn enough about our ability (free will) to choose to do GOD'S will without bad killing and to work for an end to wars and have peace on earth through population controls? We must do this before our natural resources; especially carbon fuels begin to come to an end. There are now over six billion people on earth and the population is still growing. It won't be long before it will be too late to prevent many from suffering poverty, malnutrition, and starvation, not to mention having to do without air conditioning.

One last thought and question that may not yet have an answer is; most people give little consideration to killing non-sentient organisms because they think that they cannot feel pleasure or pain. If a tree feels nothing, then chopping it down just doesn't matter to it. Is this true? I don't know. A live tree performs feats (producing fruit, etc) and a dead tree cannot. Thus, there must be some form of comfortable and uncomfortable state for plants. Do these states involve pleasure and pain? Maybe, but surely not as we understand them.

Can we get some help from the philosophers? I hope so. It seems that many if not most of the philosophers spend their time pondering the imponderable. Many spend their efforts trying to prove that there is or is not a GOD. While many more, who don't agree with each other, know the answer and spend their time either trying to prove that they are right or explaining their religious dogma. To some extent it looks like we too have been playing this game. If there is any real difference, it is that we are saying that our religion and the GOD that goes along with it are encouraging us to work on problems that are practical and can help man extend the good life (defined below) here on Earth to future generations, and to leave the hereafter to GOD'S care, hoping that in the hereafter He also abides by the golden rule. In this regard we do differ from Christianity in that although faith is necessary, it is good deeds that count the most. It is somewhat of a digression here, but some of my Christian friends believe that you are saved only through faith or belief in Christ. Good deeds alone cannot save you. These people don't seem to realize how real faith is determined. Professing belief or really believing in your heart and mind isn't enough. Faith is true only in so far as it is demonstrated! Demonstrated by good deeds that are done by following and living by the teaching of men like Christ, especially those where he is speaking as the teacher of righteous. Professed faith is not faith unless it is demonstrated. Christians who demonstrate faith most of the time but occasionally let their deeds indicate that they have lost or temporarily lost sight of their faith, feel that they have to get forgiveness for their failure so that they won't be punished for them after death. Here good deeds may differ somewhat from those we have yet to define. In any case we may not have to worry about punishment in the hereafter, because we do not yet have a hell or a bad God to go along with it.

Some of the things that philosophers consider; like ethics, morals and human nature are likely to help with our problems. We must deal with these concepts in order to get people to become better informed and to make them want to help us save the future. It would be nice to re-read the books on the History of Civilization and take notes on the history of the development of these concepts. But, at the moment there is not time for this. The following is from what notes that are at hand. Someone must have said the following. Ethics evolved out of our human nature as shaped by our social instincts and our capacity for reasoning. As social animals, we need the cooperation of our fellow human beings. As intellectual animals, we win their cooperation by defending our conduct in terms of its contribution to the common good. At first, such ethical impartiality was limited to the good of one's tribal group then to one's social group; but as the circle of social interaction expanded, people were eventually led to see that the interest of all human beings deserve, in so far as is possible, equal consideration. Concerning morals, Darwin may have said: moral sense is a joint product of the social emotions and intellectual capacities of man. We are moved by sympathies such as love, anger or hate, and guilt. Parental emotions move us to care for our children; sexual emotions move us to care for our mates; and affiliation emotions move us to care for family members and for friends with whom we have developed special bonds and our humanitarian feelings and sympathetic concerns can be extended to distant strangers. Also, we can generalize these social emotions into customary or legal rules for judging behavior as right or wrong, just or unjust. Both of the above comments on ethics and morals will be limited by any constraints that nature may have placed on the degree of obtrusions that a society may be able to promote and maintain.

What about human nature? What is it? Is it as simple as what humans will most likely do in a given situation? Is it acting on emotions without consequent reasoning? Is reasoning without emotion natural to humans? Is human nature malleable so that it can be shaped to societies needs? Can social problems be solved through a program to make human nature conform to rational norms to produce social harmony? Can conformity to human nature be used as a standard for social good? We use reason to determine how best to satisfy our desires and justify our actions, but can we use reason to move us to moral action without the motivation of our desires? Maybe not, because without emotions nothing would matter to us except, possibly, surviving. The important questions are: Does human nature manifest the uniquely human freedom to transcend nature? Can we insist on human freedom from the constraints of biological nature? Can natural tendencies such as social ranking, male dominance, sex roles, and attachment to one's kin be subjugated to the good of society even by degree? The answer is yes! If we use our souls (our free will) to chose to do so. But, we must be educated, that is to be taught the need for such actions until society is truly motivated to do so. This won't normally be the case, and when our emotions conflict, we must use practical reasoning to develop rules of action to resolve the conflict, and knowing what we must do for the well being of all future generations will help us in this regard. In addressing these conflicts we must keep in mind what we are working with, what we must abide by, and consider where modifications, if needed, can be made. At least some of these things are:

(1) Our ethical concerns manifest natural human desires.

(2) These decisions are rooted in our biological nature.

(3) Despite the variability of our moral judgments in different circumstances enduring standards of right and wrong are rooted in our natural instincts.

(4) Our problems are global but conditions at every place are not the same and solution at different places may differ in form but not in purpose.

(5) There will always be some people who may be intelligent and have the ability to reason, but, never the less they have no moral sense. This happens because they lack the social emotions (sympathy, love, guilt and shame) that support morality in normal people. Some of these people will commit acts that are incomprehensible to moral people. These cases will be the exception and must be handled separately and must not be allowed to impact the above decision-making process, nor cast doubts on its ability to succeed.

Let's try to summarize to see if we need to do more or stop here. First, we have a GOD and we have a moral code, 14 commands in all. We know how GOD communicates with men. We know that mankind is God's chosen species. He has given us a task that is to be performed here on Earth. That task is to regulate the populations of every living thing here on Earth. We are to do this through the controlled use of his natural resources and his renewable resources. We are to use our natural resources, especially our energy resources as sparingly and as efficiently as possible. Man is to maintain his own population at a level that can be afforded a good life using primarily renewable resources alone. The principal use of our energy resources will be to promote the growth and distribution of the renewable resources. Man is to think in terms not of centuries or milleniums, but in terms of hundreds of thousands, millions or even billions of years.

GOD has given man a free will (a soul) so that he can choose how conditions on Earth will be many, many eons in the future. Man has a choice, but he has to choose and there are only two choices. Currently man has chosen the evil routes. He is violating nearly all of God's commands. He is doing this through the reckless use of our natural resources in his effort at globalization. In two to four centuries he may be able to modernize more of the world, bringing what he calls the good life to more and more people while his population is allowed to continuously increase. But his, so called, progress is being obtained at the expense and to the sorrow of the generations to follow. Once the finite resources, which should be the wealth of all generations who will live on Earth, are expended the structure that globalization has built will collapse and most people will experience poverty, famine, pestilence, and death. The population level will adjust itself.

Of course this won't happen suddenly. Everyone won't wake up one morning and say, "Oh my God what have we done to cause you to punish us this way?" Our resources are large, but finite and none of us living today, including our grandchildren will live to see the beginning of the end when it becomes painfully obvious that our natural resources are really running out. At first the price of fuels will begin to rise until our economic system, which will be based on global transportation of goods, people and armies will collapse. Some people will try to get humanitarian aid to the needy for a while. Others will try to acquire, store, and horde energy sources for their own personal use. These will become the new wealthy and they will need the support a religion that keeps them alive.

Things could happen in a different way. The military of the world leaders may try to obtain control of the remaining energy resources and thereby produce a nuclear holocaust that reduces the population and may damage the environment to an extent that reduces it more.

The point is that if we don't see the light; and see it soon; our choice will have been made for us. Each generation is a generation of new souls and it gets to make a new choice. It does this by accepting things as they are or by trying to change them from their evil direction to the virtuous direction. Free will is not something that can only be used once. You can change your mind whenever the communications you receive from GOD tends to cause you to do so. It is not too late for this generation to begin the change to the virtuous route. Let's try to do it.

O.K., but how do we get started? What do we actually do? The first thing to do is to get as many people as possible to read this paper.

The second thing is to establish a focal point where those who agree in general with these teachings can communicate with each other and form an organization (a church) dedicated to spreading the gospel (good news) for all, especially those yet to be born. The commandments must be popularized and accepted.

The third thing is to enlist the best minds to help design and engineer the dwelling of the future and the transportation that is to connect then and support them.

The fourth thing is to expand the moral code into a system of laws that are designed to support and enforce God's will. The population levels per locality must be established and enforced.

The fifth thing is to promote the maximization of the quality of life at each locality. This does not mean to try to make them equal.

The sixth and maybe the most important thing is to make it understood that GOD is truly universal and here on Earth global. GOD is the GOD of everyone not just the Jews, the Christians, the Arabs, the Indians, the Chinese, etc. Each of these groups may also have their own GOD as long as their beliefs are not counter productive. They may each have their own heavens and hells and any other beliefs that don't prevent them from working now for the generations on Earth in the hereafter.

I keep saying that the other religions can have their own GODS as if this could be a facet or easily accomplished thing. However, I know that it will be just the opposite. It would require each of the other religions to modify their dogma to some extent. For example, the Christians could still have their own heaven and hell where there are only those who have been saved or damned through faith, grace, elect or the lack thereof. Something like abortion, fornication, masturbation, homosexuality, mercy killings, criminal execution and other things that are not necessarily illegal (sins) according to our 14 commandments, will have to wait for Jesus to provide punishment for violation of these commandments. To me this seems only fitting, because when the Bible says justice is mine, this means, that it is GOD, not ours. In a sense, the religions of the world tend to obey the laws of Biology. They do this in a manner similar to that of plants. Each religion is a species made up of its churches and their members. To grow, these members must breed and being members they must raise their young to be members of their species (religion). They can also grow by obtaining new members from other species by proselytization. They could also grow in a relative sense by killing off the members of the other species, but hopefully we will soon put a stop to this. This growth is to grow through competition, which is the selection process for determining the survival of the fittest. Unfortunately, each species breaks up into subspecies as sects and these sects engage as competitors among themselves for control or dominance of their species. These killings among the sects have nearly been eliminated and that sect who out breeds and best trains their off-springs to the dogma of their sect will eventually dominate. In Christianity, it seems that the Catholics are doing by far, the best job.

Each of the religions will now have to pay homage to our new religion. They may do this my recognizing it as the global religion of all or by recognizing it as the government and the civil law which all must obey. Hopefully, something like this can be peacefully achieved.

The seventh and the last, is not a day of rest. It is the understanding that these writings are only a first approximation, the results of only one persons rambling thoughts on raison d'etre. They are not infallible. They are incomplete; the laws have not been determined, the rituals that will help to hold us together have not been developed. The structure of the church has not been conceived. The form of the local governments, the states or regional governments has not been determined. How these governments are connected and subjugated is open. There are thousands of things yet to be done before we will be able to make an impact on history. Getting many people in nearly every country on Earth to consider these thoughts can be the first step in helping man to choose to join God on the road to a good future for man for as long as man is allowed to exist on Earth.

When I started recording these thoughts, my objective was to try to give an answer to the question "What is the reason or justification for existence? I tried to do that without relying on my Christian upbringing for the answers. To do this I had to assume that Christianity is no more or less valid than any of the other great religions of history. I had no conscious preconceived opinion of what the outcome would be. My first thought was that there have been many Gods and more religions so why not make up one more, one that is created specifically to answer the question of "reason d'etre. The above is a record of this effort. You be the judge of its logic and its results.

Of course, I am now biased, for me the God and the religion alluded to above is far better than any to which I have been previously exposed. It may happen that someone may say, "But Tom, this is only another description of such and such a God." In that case, all that I can say is well maybe there really is nothing new under the sun. But, as Patrick Henry might have said, "If this be new or not new, let's make the most of it: as for me, give me this God or give me the consequences of not having one." There are people who have wondered why (not being a Christian) I am so honest. If they were to ask me, I would tell them because it makes me feel better. There is something about this God that is very much like honesty.

I have had these thoughts and now I pray that you men and women, who can, will take it farther and do some good with it. This will surely make you feel better.

If you have read this far, I wish to thank you. You are a true friend. If you do more, I wish to praise you; you will have earned it and the praise of those yet to come. I believe that you will also earn God's thanks and rewards in his heaven of which he has yet to tell us.

# EPILOGUE

It was not intended, but this effort has turned out to be somewhat in the form of an Epic Drama which is a narrative drama that seeks to provoke critical thoughts about social or in this case religious problems by appealing to the reader's reason rather than his emotions. This may have made it seem that our religion is not mystical, that is has no mystique and worse of all that, unlike nearly all other religions, it contains no miracles. Nothing could be further from the truth!

Mystical means of, relating to, or, resulting from an individual's direct communications with GOD, or ultimate reality. Our religion is more mystical that any other religion. The Christian Religion, for example, began when God communicated with Paul in a dream. The results produced by this dream, is one of histories most remarkable miracles. To make this miracle what it is today; God had to also communicate with Constantine and thereby make him an efficient killer in the name of Christ and to make Christianity the religion of the Roman Nations. The backing of the military force let to the establishment of Christianity as one of the world's great religions. I am not sure but after Constantine the Christian GOD may have stopped communicating with man, but man has yet to learn this. I feel this way because the overall record of the Popes seems to indicate that it is true. Our miracles, unlike the mythical miracles found in the holy books but not in other works of "factual" history, - are true miracles, in the sense that they are also a part of factual history.

These miracles have resulted from God's communication with all men at all times. The miracles have not resulted from one or two men hearing GOD at critical times, but from many thousands of men, not only hearing GOD, as we all can if we try, but learning more about GOD and how he does things. We have learned much from the people who have studied math, physics, chemistry, hydrocarbon chemistry, biochemistry, biology, microbiology, medical arts, engineering botany and political science and practices, etc. In political practices alone we have learned that governments can exist and thrive where the government is answerable to the people, where rule is by the rule of law and all are subject to the law, a law that provides for and protects the basic rights of all people, a law that can also provide for equal or nearly equal educational opportunities. If there is anyone who does not think that this is truly a miracle and truly mystical, let him imagine how he could explain this, say, 400 years ago and make anyone believe that he was not inspired by GOD or insane. If we had known 2000 years ago what we so far have learned about GOD, then we could have determined if Christ's DNA differs in anyway from other men or if he was really a descendant from David. We would be able to tell if anyone who might claim to be Christ at his Second Coming is lying or not.

The above discussion is not intended to indicate that science is the new religion and scientists its priests. However, the sciences do tend to sum up what we think we understand about what GOD is trying to tell us and to help us listen with a keener ear and to look for a better understanding. Those things that we do learn are in and of themselves neither good nor bad. They are just a few of the infinite facets of GOD. However, the manner in which man makes use of this knowledge can be either bad or good. Let's choose to believe that using this knowledge of GOD to help GOD preserve all of his species for all times, or for at least as long as possible is good. Let this be our faith.

GOD talks to us and like children we can and do talk back. We talk to GOD through our actions. GOD hears us and lets things happen according to these our prayers. You see we also talk to GOD all the time. Most of the time we do this unconsciously. We can and should also pray consciously. When we do, let us try to remove our self as far as we can from all things other than our thoughts of GOD. Then let us begin by saying "God thy will be done!" We don't start this way to try to tell him something that he doesn't already know. We are trying to tell him that we also know and understand. "I thank thee for blessing me." This means giving me a soul, a free will, an opportunity to help determine how things here on Earth will transpire. "Deliver me from evil..." This means let me not be a glutton or be wasteful, and to not unnecessarily increase the population. "Guide me in the way of righteousness." This means let me try to live, in so far as possible, on our renewable resources alone. "Do this so that I may be of service to both you and to all of your creations". This means to help me to live an exemplary life that inspires others to emulate me. "I understand that thy will be merciful or revengeful." This means that man can learn to make do with what he has or he can use it up, destroy it, and thereby destroy his own comfort and maybe himself. "I pray that by my example, enough will follow to make mercy happen, forever and ever; Amen."

> *God, thy will be done!*
> *I, thank you for blessing me.*
> *Deliver me from evil.*
> *Guide me in the way righteousness.*
> *Do this so that I can be of service to both you and to all of your cre-*
> *ations.*
> *I understand that thy will be merciful or revengeful.*
> *I pray that by my example, enough will follow to make mercy happen,*
> *Forever and ever,*
> > *Amen.*

Now that I think I know our reason for existence, I feel helpless. I am now a young 72. What can I, one individual, do to help justify our existence? I can and I shall father no more children, nor do anything else to encourage the growth of the population. I have already set examples, good and bad, for all of my children from both of my marriages, and I am trying to set good examples for my grandchildren. I have neither hindered nor encouraged their religious activities. The example here has been to do unto others, as you would have them do unto you. I hope that if and when they read these thoughts, they will realize that this GOD is reconcilable with their current beliefs whatever they may be. These things I shall continue to do. Where

I feel helpless is when I try to consider how can mankind be made to or encouraged to change the manner in which we use our natural resources especially gas, oil and coal. This truly is a staggering task. Capitalism and the free enterprise system will have to take on a new meaning. "Good times" cease to depend on economic expansion produced by continuing globalization of the underdeveloped countries and growth in the population. World travel for fun and education will have to come to a near stop. Education about other places, people and customs will be obtained through computers and the media as it does for most of us today. When the population becomes stabilized so will the economy. However, people will not change in that men will not be equal, as they were not created equal. Hopefully legal protection and educational opportunities will be as equal as possible. But some men will be more talented, quick to learn, study harder, or just inherit wealth. These men will come to run the governments, the industries, the social, the entertainment, and the religious functions. Wealth will still be accumulated, but hopefully, to a much lesser extent than it is today. It is also hoped that these rich are faithful members of our religion and will accept the responsibility of extending the life of our natural resources. Life for the future generations will not be Amish-like. There will always be challenges and more to learn. This is especially true concerning our knowledge of GOD.

The solution is simple, however the implementation may be impractical but let's hope not impossible. Let's hope that human nature will not prevent us from obtaining a good approximation. I thank GOD for giving us the chance and pray that mankind will join together and join with GOD to make mercy happen. My only regret is that I did not get an earlier start and have so little time left to try to do more. Praise be unto GOD.

After writing these thoughts and being able to read them in type, I have afterthoughts. How does this differ from the teachings of Thomas R. Malthus? I looked up Malthus in the dictionary, and found that Thomas said that the population tends to increase at a rate faster than its means of subsistence and unless it (the population growth) is checked by moral restraints or by disease, famine, war, or other disasters, poverty will spread and degradation inevitably result. Well now, it looks like old Thomas was on the right track, but he was before the era of carbon fuels. Once our carbon fuels are squandered, the population growth will not only be stopped but it will be reversed until equilibrium is reached that can be maintained by our ability to manage and increase our renewable resources. The only time in history that the population growth has been reversed (as far as I know) was during the Black Plague. Wars don't do it. Only pestilence such as plagues and famine work. It has been said that God works in mysterious ways. This is not so, for the above ways of GOD are not mysterious. He has granted us the power to make mercy happen. Let's do it.

You see we thought that we could just make up another GOD, but instead we discovered the only true GOD. The only one that made us has told us how he made us, and continues to educate us in his ways. Including ways in which we can join with GOD to help bring about the future. All of the other Gods were made by man for mans benefit either here or in the hereafter. Man had absolutely nothing to do with the making of this GOD. GOD made man and everything else and he has blessed man above all things. Man and only man can choose to work with GOD to choose the direction of things to come. Again let's thank GOD and work to make mercy happen.

Well, we have a god, but we don't have a name for our religion, church or government to be, and what happened to the Devil? For starters let's call our religion, church and our government – **PARTNERS WITH GOD FOR MERCY**.

What may have become the Devil may be that part of mankind who are not members of PARTNERS WITH GOD FOR MERCY. They, by not choosing to join with us, have willingly or unwillingly become **PARTNERS WITH GOD FOR EVIL!**

Maybe Isaiah (45:7 King James) understood this when he had GOD say "I formed the light, and created darkness: I made the peace, and created evil: I the Lord do all these things!" We must accept that in our GOD there is not only the source of all that we call good, but there is also the source of all that we call evil. This helps explain how and why GOD is both merciful and revengeful, and why we don't have, nor need a devil.

Our religion must become an instrument for governmental rule, a rule that dominates all the people of the world for the future good of all. Our religion, our faith is no different than every other faith in so far as it offers freedom and calls for obedience, the acceptance of authority, and the surrender of the self for the good of a future existence. However, our future existence is here on Earth and it is the existence of all of our descendants.

I wish that I knew how the revolution or revolutions that will establish this new government could or will be brought about. It seems that, it may, in some cases, occur from the top down as when a despot might be converted and bring his people with him as was the case with Constantine and Christianity. In other cases from the bottom up, by convincing the electorate in a democracy to modify, if necessary, their constitution to allow this to happen. It may be more realistic to try to win over the free countries and have them coalesce into one government that will be strong enough to cause most of the other countries to join up. If enough of them do, then it may become possible to force the others without the use of weapons of mass destruction, which is the last way that we will want to reduce the population level.

Our reasoning, logically we hope, has led us to a government that appears to be a theocracy and history has indicated that whenever a religious creed, the military, the Judiciary, and the police are in partnership, man becomes a slave. When man is enslaved, government is overthrown and a different form is set up. Theocracies, especially, don't seem to last. "Historically, the liberty of man has not been safe in the hands of the church."

Why then should we expect that in our case that history wouldn't be repeated? Well, theology is a superstition, humanist is a religion and all previous theocracies have been based on a myth that could not tolerate other theologies and could be maintained only so long as enlightenment could be suppressed. Our religion is based on humanism of the finest kind; enlightenment is encouraged and supported. Enlightenment will help our government to survive as long as the Earth can be made to support life. Enlightenment will continue to raise doubts in the minds of members of the other faiths that are tolerated. Their membership will tend to decrease. But we know that we will never know all there is to know about GOD so there may always be those who need to believe, through faith alone, in a particular kind of heaven and even a hell if they choose.

We will never be able to change and channel human nature to suit our needs and we would not want to. We will always want man to be intellectually free. We want him to question everything. In essence, this is how we listen to and learn about GOD, and the more we know about GOD the more we will become better partners. Most of the existing religions, whose dogma was set in the past, are threatened by every newly learned truth. With each new truth, they die a little and eventually they will all die. However, our dogma is always developing and it is our job to have everyone to understand and to believe!

Some philosophers ask questions like 'what is matter?' And then arrive at answers that are totally absurd, that mean nothing and are worthless. They should have asked 'what does matter?' Then maybe their answer could be summarized by the last sentence in Bertrand Russell's book – *The ABC of Relativity* - "*The final conclusion is that we know very little, and yet it is astonishing that we know so much, and still more astonishing that so little knowledge can give so much power*". Let's use this power to make mercy happen!

I have recently found in some of my old notes, the following information. I am not sure of the source, but it most likely is from one of the books by Will Durant. A man named Pico Della Mirandula, writing in Florence in the late 15th Century, before Columbus discovered America said: 'And then Pico put into the mouth of GOD himself, as words spoke to Adam, a divine Testimony to the limitless potentialities of man:' "*I created thee as being neither heavenly nor earthly – that thou mightest be free to shape and to overcome thyself. Thou mayest sink into a beast or be born anew to the divine likeness.*"

'To this Pico added:' "This is the culminating gift of GOD, this is the supreme and marvelous felicity of man.... that he can be that which he wills to be. Animals, from the moment of their birth carry with them, from their mother's bodies, all that they are destined to have or to be: the highest spirits (angels) are from the beginning .... what they will be forever. But GOD the Father endowed man from birth with the seeds of every possibility and every life."

What could be more beautiful? This belongs in the ancient history part of our Bible whenever it becomes to be written.

History belongs to heroes and to be sure that the heroes are not forgotten, history tends to become mythology, or vice versa, and it happens like the end of Camelot, where it says "Don't let it be forgot. That once there was a spot, for one brief shining moment that was known as Camelot." However, in either case, this spot and the moment were in the past. But now the heroes will be the partners with GOD for mercy; the spot will be the entire earth; the moment will be in the future and it will last for as long as GOD intended.

# Post Script

I stopped writing The Rambling Thoughts in 2001 and I wrote the Epilogue in early 2002. I stopped because I did not want to push on toward what I felt would be the logical conclusion, which would suggest the final solution. The final solution would be to have one world government whose main purpose would be to own, operate and control the distribution of all of our natural resources. This world government would also control the use of these resources. In addition to this, they would establish and enforce the laws that set the various population levels and insure that the 14 commandments are obeyed.

It is difficult to see how this may be brought about in a timely manner. However, great changes may have begun on September 11, 2001 when dastardly and very effective terrorist attacks on New York City and Washington, DC were carried out by followers of Osamar Bin Laden and the Taliban government of Afghanistan. President Bush used these events to have Congress grant him something like wartime powers to wage a campaign (which is called a war) on terrorism, wherever it may be found. Of course, we know that real terror consists of two main aspects. The first is the ability to use weapons of mass destruction against us and the second is the likelihood that they will be used.

Weapons of mass destruction that are of primary concern are conventional, nuclear, chemical and biological. One who has those weapons and also has the ability to deliver them is a potential threat. If he is also a potential enemy then he is a constant threat. If he is an enemy, then he is an eminent threat. One who might have any one of these weapons or may be trying to develop them is a possible threat and may become a threat.

Using the above criteria, then who are the dangerous terrorist that have these weapons and the ability to use them against us? We can make a list of whom we have to watch and whom we need to make preemptive strikes against.  If we were to do this, we would include names like Russia, China, France, Israel, India, Pakistan and others.  Then we would make a list of those who are trying to acquire enough material to make one or more bombs.  This list would definitely include North Korea and possibly others.  The next list would be those who would very much like to have one of these weapons.  Iraq would head this list.  But, I believe that Iraq does not have any of these weapons and is not likely to get any unless maybe China, France or North Korea was to sell them one.  What if this happened?  They would still not have the means to use it against the United States.  Therefore if we are to make a preemptive strike against anyone, it should be made against North Korea.  It should be made as soon as possible and without any negotiations or warnings.

NOTE that Afghanistan, Osamar Bin Laden and Al-Qaida did not make any of the lists, yet they have been the only ones to make successful mass destructive attacks.  Why did this happen?  It happened because the above description of what constitutes a terrorist is incomplete.  It does not include those who are willing and happy to die in the act of accomplishing terror.  These people don't have to have any large bombs, nuclear, chemical, or biological weapons.  They are able through deception and cunning coupled with total religious faith to use our resources against us, and the event of 9-11 is the best example of this.  The Taliban in Afghanistan had conventional weapons, but these were used primarily to control their own people in a police state, which is a type of local terror.  Even though they would have liked to have weapons of mass destruction and be able to use them, they did not have any.  They primarily used things like truck bombs or large airplanes with fully loaded fuel tanks.  In this last case they managed to use our planes not their own.  It seems to me that their modus operandi has been to wait one to two years after a successful terror attach before another one was attempted.  Thus, if their operation has not been completely disrupted then it is about time for another attack, (which will be against America or its possessions, if possible) to occur.

All of this has led President Bush to somehow decide that the next battle in the "war" against terrorism should be fought against Iraq instead of North Korea which is clearly where it should start.  Neither of these two countries is capable of attacking the U.S. from their homeland. But North Korea has the where-with-all to make nuclear bombs and Iraq does not. Then why attack Iraq first? Of course, I do not know all of the facts, but the following seems to be some of the reasons:

(1) Historically the country that has, or thinks it has, the greatest military powers, eventually finds that it must wage war. Wars for which they think that they are superbly equipped. If these military powers have been maintained and improved over a considerable time without experiencing combat, then these wars will be started or provoked under circumstances and contingencies that would be, not only ill-advised and undesirable, but objectionable.

(2) The existence of Sadam Hassein in power in Iraq is somewhat of an embarrassment for the Bush Family.

(3) There is oil and a lot of it in Iraq. This oil can be used to help pay for restoring the damages done by the war, pay for our cost of the war and pay for improving the living conditions of the people of Iraq (those that survive the war – that is).

(4) Here our armed forces directed by our Commander-in-Chief can again demonstrate to the world just how much our new technological weapons are superior to anything that Iraq can field.

(5) It is felt that Sadam can be removed from power quickly and without "too" many loses on our side.

(6) We should be able to get the UN behind us on this move whereas it may be more difficult to get the UN to sanctify the blowing up of North Korea's reactor.

(7) I have thought that George Bush was an aggressive, active religious hypocrite for political gain. However, it might be that he is a religious fanatic who sees himself as a profit of God who is to lead a holy crusade against Iraq, Islam and the Middle East for the sake of democracy, Christianity, the God of all mankind and especially the poor subjugated people of the Middle East, and;

(8) All of this may be timed so as to lead to Bush's election in 2004; after all he only won the last election in the courts.

It may be a coincident, but oil might also have been a consideration in the seemingly successful attack on the Taliban Government in Afghanistan. It seems that a pipeline across Afghanistan may be the cheapest way to bring the oil north of Afghanistan to market.

Well, what has all of this to do with Rambling Thoughts? In order for the New World government to control the distribution and use of the natural resources, they must first gain control of them. This will require that all governments, where these resources reside, give up their sovereignty at least in so far as energy resources are concerned and with human nature being as it is, this probably can not be accomplished without the use of force. Therefore, a group of the most powerful nations need to adapt our religion and thereby give up part of their sovereignty. Then our combined forces, hopefully through threats, will be used to gain and hold control throughout the world.

However, while all of this is being accomplished we must never forget that we are always working for the mercy of all. We must also remember the important lessons that were taught to us by those ancients who were in essence, tuned to us and were also partners with GOD for mercy. Two of these lessons are: (1) from the prophet Micah – "All that the Lord requires is that you treat others with justice, to love mercy, and to walk humbly with your GOD." And (2) from Jesus Christ – "The greatest commandment is to love GOD and the second is to love one's neighbor as one's self, and on these two commandments hang all the laws of the prophets."

This list could and should be made longer. Maybe later it will be, but for now we must realize that when trying to keep true to these lessons we may not be able to avoid all violence. Doing acts of violence to others, whom we are supposed to and are trying to love, has been and may always be a problem, on the local, national and international levels. Let's hope that by trying to be good partners, we may eliminate this problem, at least on the large-scale beginning with wars. Maybe one day our tanks, war planes, and battle ships (modern swords) can be turned into instruments for helping to nurture mankind (modern plow shares).

I have recently read a couple of philosophy books and one of the things that I think I have learned is that they play games with the definitions of words. For example, take the words art and artist. It seems that art is such a simple thing, but what is art truly?

"Well what truly is something as simple as art?"

"True art is the revelation of truth."

"What is truth?"

"Truth is something that reveals essence – that is true nature."

"Here we go again – what is essence?"

"The essence of any and everything is part of God, and the infinite sum of all essence is GOD."

"In the beginning was the word; the word was with God and the word was essence."

"Art is those things the realization of which makes us human – GOD made us that way."

"Therefore, GOD is the ultimate artist and here on Earth, mankind is his greatest work."

"Let's help keep it that way."

# Post Script II

It is now 3 March 2004.  I have just finished reading two books.  The first was by Keith Hopkins, a Christian Historian; the title is "A World Full of Gods – The Strange Triumph of Christianity".  This book goes a long way toward demythologizing Christian dogma.  The second book by John Shelby Spong, an Episcopalian (Anglican) Bishop and now a lecturer at Harvard University, entitled, "Why Christianity Must Change or Die" finishes the job.  He makes Christianity unbelievable for anyone whose mind is even slightly open.  The reason for recording this information here is that after killing the Theistic Gods, Spong tries to retain what is left of Jesus to resurrect from the remains of Christianity, a new religion for what he calls believers in Exile.  He even tries to envision what the churches and the new church services will be like.  In chapter eleven – The Emerging Church: reading the signs present today and in Chapter twelve – The Future Church: a speculative dream, he lays out his plan for accomplishing this.

It was not our intention in the beginning to produce a faith that eliminated our need to attend church, but, so far our church only has a name, no meeting places and no services.  The above plan could be adapted to our purposes and maybe Spong could be encouraged to help.  Maybe he could extend this plan to be adaptable to any and all of the existing religions.

The main reason that Rambling Thoughts has not yet been published is that I have not yet been able to obtain permission to copy the three chapters from The Lessons of History.  I have tried to write so that this material could be omitted.  But if it is omitted, the reader will not see the material that most influenced my thoughts, because I cannot expect each reader to also buy a copy of the Lessons of History.

While I was waiting to get permission to use the copyrighted material, I read volume I of Joseph Campbell's book, "The Masks of God".  This book is essentially a scientific study of mythology.  My copy of this book contains

472 pages of text. The short last section (Conclusion – The Functioning of Myth) ends with the following sentences "For the human mind in it's polarity of the male and female modes of experience, in its passage from infancy to adulthood and to old age, in its toughness and tenderness, and in its continuing dialogue with the world, is the ultimate myth genetic zone – the creator and destroyer, the slave and yet the master of all the GODS". If Joseph could read this work, I feel that he would say his conclusions have again been verified.

In the final analysis, I would like to say the following to Milton Howie:

Dear Milt, I know that this is not the answers that you expected or wanted. They also may not be very good answers but they are the best that I could do, and I want to sincerely thank you for causing me to have these thoughts. Lets both hope that they do more good than harm or do nothing.

Actually, I have not changed things as much as you may think. For example consider these words from the first book of your bible:

> And GOD made the two great lights; the greater light to rule the day, and the lesser light to rule the night; he made the stars also. And GOD set them in the firmament of heaven to give light upon the earth.
>
> And GOD said let the earth bring forth the living creature after its kind, cattle and creeping things, and beast of the earth after its kind: and it was so.
>
> And GOD said, let us make man in our image, after our likeness: and let them have dominion over the fish of the sea, and over the fowl of the air, and over the cattle, and over all the earth, and over every creeping thing that creepeth upon the earth. – Gen. I.

We have not eliminated nor changed these words. They are still true – all of them, also the words of Isaiah (45.7) "I form the light, and create darkness; I make peace, and create evil, I the Lord do all these things!" These words are not only true, but they now make sense. These words and many others will be part of our Bible when it is written. However, these words only tell us what GOD did and why GOD did it – that is what God assigned man (to be read mankind) to do.  But, now we know a lot about how GOD did these things and we have chosen and recommended one way to go about achieving GOD's assignment.  This recommendation is not complete, nor static.  It will continue to be modified as we are able to hear and understand what GOD is saying to us and we can be assured that he is God and will always be talking to us.

In a sense the earth is a host and all living things are parasites, either on the earth itself or on each other.  We are all relatives; products of Mother Earth and we should love each other.  This is difficult because we are all greedy and struggle to obtain more than our share from Mother Earth.  The ecology changes as the result of this struggle and as a result of natural phenomena.  Parts of the nourishments of Mother Earth are finite and as these are used up, the host becomes incapable of maintaining all species.  The only species capable of extending the lifetime of these nourishments is mankind and it is GOD'S desire for man to do so.

I heard this philosophy being discussed while watching a Native American Indian Religious Teacher explaining his beliefs on a television program.  It is a different way of saying what I have attempted to present in this book.

One afterthought, it seems that H. G. Wells was right when he said history is more and more becoming a "race between education and catastrophe", and currently it seems that education is falling behind.  If you can, please help.

About 100 years ago TOLSTOY who tried to found a new religion called TOLTOYISM was in his eighties and near the end of his life.  At that time he was sick and in delirium.   When he came out of delirium he asked his daughter to write down a few thoughts on GOD that had come to him during his delirium.  He then said with his voice hoarse and gasping: "GOD is that infinite whole of which man is conscious of being a finite part.  Man is his manifestation in matter, space and time."  It took Tolstoy nearly all of his life to find the right starting place.  It is unfortunate that he did not have time to give it more thought.  We now know very much more about that infinite whole and are working to learn more.  (Tolstoy by Henri Troyat, Doubleday and Company, Inc. (1997, Page 712).

One of the Buddhist proverbs is "To everyone is given the key to the gates of heaven; the same key opens the gates of hell." This key is your soul and your freewill.    You can use it to open the gates to the Partners with God for Mercy or to become a partner with GOD for evil!

It has been said that science is necessarily rational and religion is irrational. If it were otherwise, we could reconcile the innate foolishness and cruelties of man with the infinite wisdom of GOD.  Since morality and inspiration are based on faith or agreement, they are irrational and are not part of the subject matter of science.  Everyone, including scientist can agree and no conflicts need arise.  However, the metaphysical aspects are different and conflicts will arise.  Here science can't change; religion being irrational may or may not change as it so desires.

# APPENDIX A

(Continued from Page 13)

Are these GODS and their models of the beginnings of the universe just myths? Well let's see how the word myth is defined. My dictionary gives seven definitions, as follows:

(1) Usually: Traditional stories of ostensibly historical events that serve to unfold part of the worldview of a people or explain a practice, belief or natural phenomenon.

(2) Parable: Allegory.

(3) A person or thing having only an imaginary or unverifiable existence.

(4) An ill-founded belief held uncritically especially by an interested group.

(5) A story that makes sense within its own terms, offers explanations for everything we can see around us, but can be neither tested not disproved.

(6) A myth is an explanation that people agree on because it is convenient to agree on it, not because its truth can be demonstrated.

(7) The whole body of myths.

Well it seems that all religions are myths. These religious myths include all the various explanations of "*In the beginning there was....*" Therefore the physical theories of creation are also myths, but they differ somewhat from the others in that the, so-called, fundamental principles upon which it is and will be founded can be demonstrated or tested. This does not mean that all the fundamental laws needed to explain the BIG BANG THEORY (BBT) are known or that all of the ones that we think we know have been completely verified. Also when new laws for the high energy physics part of the cosmological theories are proposed, the laboratory accelerators to test these laws do not exist and because of cost and size, they may never exist here on Earth. This is especially true for predicting what may have happened during the first very small fractions of a second in the big bang.

The BBT is not complete. Among other things, it does not explain the particle anti-particle asymmetry. There should be just as many anti-particles as particles. But there seems to be only particles. If we want anti-particles, we have to expend energy to make them. Also where did the energy for the BBT came from and why it came at this time or at all is truly mystical, even more so than a GOD appearing here on Earth for a short while and then disappearing. Also, there are other holes in it. For example, why is the Universe not only expanding but seems to be expanding at an accelerating rate? Cosmologists do not mind proposing anti-gravitational forces, like dark matter with anti-gravity properties to explain this. At first this seemed to me to be ludicrous, especially when they don't try to explain how this dark matter came to be or where it happened to be at times near zero.

Let's not limit ourselves. Let's try to improve the (BBT) myth so as to close some of these holes and make it more complete.

Richard Feynman said, if you want to change a physical theory, you can start at any point. You don't have to start at the beginning and change everything. However he did not mean that you couldn't start over if you wanted to.

Let's take a look at the BBT and see where we want to start. When did the Big Bang start? Even before there was a BBT, Cosmologists knew that the universe was very old, very big and expanding. The Earth is thought to be about five billion years old and the universe is thought to be 15 or 20 billion years old. But the BBT is only 58 years old. You see this myth is quite young. The Big Band occurred in 1946 in the mind of George Gamow (Phys. Rev.70, 572 (1946). His hypothesis was that in the beginning, there was an extremely hot and highly compressed neutron ball, bathed in radiation. This primordial fireball contained everything that there was. He called this ball, the YLEM which is an obsolete noun meaning "the primordial substance from which the elements were formed." Something (GOD?) caused the YLEM to violently expand (blow up), which caused it to cool. In a very small part of a second it had cooled enough to allow some of the neutrons to decay into protons and electrons. This started the nucleus synthesis that was supposed to produce all of the elements that we know today and some that we don't know because they have all decayed away. Using what was known of nuclear (sub atomic) physics at that time, Gamow was able to account for the production of

$$_1H^1, \ _1D^2, \ _1T^3, \ _2He^3, \ _2He^4, \ _2Be^8, \ _6C^{12}, \ _8O^{16}, \ _{10}Ne^{20}, \ _{11}Na^{23}, \ _{12}Mg^{24},$$
$$_{14}Si^{28}, \ _{15}P^{31},$$ etc. up to the elements with atomic numbers <42.

To try to explain how the first stars were formed of primarily hydrogen plus a little helium and collapsed into a fire ball, something like our sun in which an equilibrium is reached where the energy radiated away at the surface is replaced with the energy created by exothermic nuclear fusion reactions occurring in its interior would take up too much space and lead us too far afield, especially since we do not want to change this part of the theory. But very briefly for stars as large as or a little larger than our sun, the elements up to oxygen may be produced. To produce the heavy elements, the interior temperature must be higher. That is, these stars must be larger than say 10 or more times the size of our sun. Elements up to iron can be produced in exothermic fusion reactions, but the heavier the element, the higher the temperature and the bigger the star needs to be. Iron is the 56th element. We have 103 elements. The other 47 elements may be produced in endothermic fusion reactions. These reactions take up energy and tend to reduce the temperature inside the star. Stars large enough to produce temperatures high enough to drive these reactions are cooled both by radiation from their surfaces and from endothermic reactions within and both are balanced by exothermic reactions in the interiors. These stars have to develop, live, decay and die in something like a small local big bang – a supernova that creates a large stellar cloud that may still be mostly hydrogen and helium but will also contain a little of the heavy elements that were created before its death. Within this cloud, new younger stars can be created. Stars like our sun with solar systems that may contain planets maybe even one like our Earth. This may help one understand why our solar system is only

5 or 6 billion years old and how there can also be other stars in our galaxy that are more than 12 billion years old.

Why did it take so long for someone to come up with the BBT?  The BBT occurred when it did because it was not until this time that enough was known about subatomic physics to allow it to be applied (at least in thought) to an attempted explanation of cosmological observations.  Up to this time the high-energy physicists did their thing.  They built bigger and more powerful accelerators to probe the inside of the nucleons.  In a sense, they were learning more and more about less and less – that is smaller and smaller particles.  While the cosmologists learned less and less about more and more – that is they were building telescopes of all kinds to see further back in time.  When Gamow published the BBT, he created a kind of marriage between these two groups.  The marriage turned out to be a great benefit for both groups.  Without Gamow's invention, both groups would probably be out of business by now.  The chances of building the size machines needed to make further progress in High Energy Particle Physics are slim to none.  They will no longer be able to verify their theories in the laboratory.  Also, the chances that cosmologists will be able to experimentally verify their theories are the same, but together, they can continue to investigate what may have happened "in the beginning" at least theoretically.  They have worked themselves into the same box that Aristotle deliberately put himself in. Aristotle would not try to think outside of this box and the high-energy physicists, cosmologist's team, because of prohibited costs, may not be allowed to.  This situation is explained very well in a book entitled "*The End of Physics by David Lindley*".

To account for where the needed energy for the Big Bang came from, we will need to start where Gamow did – in the beginning.  We will try to start so that we not only create the needed energy in the right amount, but we will also account for lack of antiparticles.  We will begin with two particles an YLEM and an anti-YLEM.  The YLEM is composed of the primordial substance from which particles are made and the anti-YLEM, of course, is composed of the substance from which anti-particles are made.  Both the YLEM and the anti-YLEM are very massive (therefore light and any similar forms of energy, if there are any, do not escape) but finite. However, they do not contain equal amounts of mass. The anti-YLEM is smaller.

Because of their masses, they are attracted toward each other and because they are the only things in the universe, they collide. All of the anti-matter annihilates an equal amount of matter producing exactly the required energy and leaving exactly the amount of matter required for producing the universe.

You now see why there are no anti-particles roaming around all over the place. In a sense, they still exist, but as either electromagnetic energy or possibly somewhere down inside the nucleus of the elements. Maybe some of them have found a way to survive by participating in the potential energy that gives rise to the strong forces in the nucleus. We borrowed energy from these anti-particles to get things started and we can buy them back if we are willing to pay the cost in energy. The high-energy physics community has been able to pay the cost to reproduce many of these anti-particles; but presently they are out of funds for producing more.

You might ask where did this second particle come from. It came from where the first particle came. But what about time? Did time begin before the Big Bang? For us time is a sequence of events. Time is that thing which GOD invented to keep everything from happening at once. Therefore, time began when these two particles came together and for us time flows only in one direction. In physics this direction is determined by the concept of entropy. Entropy is something like the reciprocal of the total amount of energy that is available with which you can do something. As energy is used up, entropy increases and time flows in the direction of increasing entropy. To me this indicates that the universe will eventually run down, comes to equilibrium and stays there. It will not again collapse on itself and create another YLEM and even if it did it won't blow up again unless it encounters another anti-YLEM, which would surely have to be supplied by GOD. However, GOD may supply another anti-YLEM, but this time maybe the anti-YLEM will be larger and an anti-universe with anti-people would be created.

To my simple mind, it is not at all certain that anti-galaxies do not exist at the current time. It seems to me that when two YLEMs collide, they don't completely overlap or thoroughly mix before they are blown apart. It could happen that only enough matter and anti-matter was annihilated to stop the two YLEMS and blow the remaining matter away in opposite directions, thus producing anti-matter galaxies on one side of the universe and matter galaxies on the other side.

In this case, if the contractions of the universe were to occur, then the fire works will be quite different and the resulting universe would also be different from the one we know.

It would be easy to reason that the above did not happen because in this case there would be something like an equatorial plane in the universe where there would be no stars, and it now seems to us that the stars are distributed uniformly in space. However, we may not have yet seen all of the universe and if our universe in something like the surface of a balloon that is expanding and constantly producing more space, then the equatorial plane may not be visible from every point in the universe.

It is also difficult for me to accept without misgivings, the relativist description of our four-dimensional space-time universe. Especially, the analogy that it is similar to the surface of a balloon that is expanding into space at a uniform, decreasing or accelerating rate. The stars and galaxies are supposed to be like dots and blotches on the surface. They should all be moving away from each other at the same rate. This makes the question "where is the center of the universe?" meaningless, because every point on this surface is in some sense, the center of the universe. (Maybe the church was right about the Earth being at the center, after all, you see if the universe stops expanding, and contracts, then all parts will become one in the end). However, the galaxies are not moving away from each other, on the contrary they seem to be moving toward each other. The galaxies collect into groups. These groups collect into clusters and the clusters collect into clusters of clusters and so on. These distributions can probably be explained using Newton's law of gravitation, which should work on these large scales. In some groups, galaxies are already colliding and here gravity causes a real mess. This makes it look more like the universe is collapsing, at least on a very large scale, but in some sense a local scale.

As we make more and more astronomical observations, cosmology becomes more and more like the Bible. In that, there are enough observations so that by picking and choosing, a cosmologist may be able to prove any-thing that he might propose.

Every physicist understands that the system of equations for explain-ing a complicated physical phenomena, especially one as complicated as our universe, has an infinite number of solutions. Special solutions are obtained by establishing or specifying boundary values or initial conditions. But when it comes to the BBT, there seems to be an aversion to changing the initial conditions or to mess with them in any way. It seems to me that this started with Paul Dirac's theory of the electron. This theory predicted the need for the existence of the positron – the first anti-particle. The position was found and this let to the production of many other anti-particles and revealed the particle – anti-particle anti-asymmetry problem.

I am not smart enough to appreciate the reasons for this aversion to changing the initial conditions. If an anti-asymmetry exists now, why not assume that it has always existed. This is what was done in the above ex-ample. Now we also have the problem of the universe expanding at an ac-celerating rate. Here we should ask our self, what were the relative sizes of the YLEM and the anti-YLEM?

The observable matter in the universe seems to be only a small fraction of the total matter. The rest is called dark matter, because it is not directly observable. However, a little of it can be detected through its effects on the motions of other observable matter. The rest, which is most of the matter, should be called mysterious matter. To try to make this matter less mysteri-ous, let's assume that both the YLEM and the anti-YLEM were much larger than the now observable matter and that the YLEM and the anti-YLEM were approximately equal – say to within 10 per cent of each other.

Then all of the anti-matter and most of matter was annihilated producing energy whose equivalent mass would be about ten times that of the observ-able matter in our universe. This energy would be of a radiative like nature in that it is moving at or near the speed of light and may have produced the so-called inflationary expansion and then left the remaining matter behind. Since this energy is traveling at or near the speed of light it produces a dark matter wave. The visible universe expands somewhat slower, but it expands faster than if it were expanding into free space. The gravity of the massive dark matter wave is pulling it along. The universe travels through space that has been prepared for it and at a seemingly accelerated rate. I believe that all of this is supposed to mean that the cosmological constant is greater than one and that the vacuum energy density is greater than one. Here I am thinking of the vacuum as that part of space that is between our universe and the expanding dark matter wave. Beyond the dark matter wave there is nothing. Thus, the universe is open and expanding. The vacuum energy density will never fall to zero.

Maybe Plato was right when he said to Socrates – "If they, Socrates, in many respects concerning many things - the GODS and the generations of the universe – we prove unable to render an account at all points consistent with itself and exact, you must not be surprised. If we can furnish accounts no less likely than any other, we must be content."

Before Copernicus, Galileo, Kepler, and Newton, GOD's creations – The Earth, the planets and the Celestial Sphere – were for mankind. The Earth was the center of the universe and man being in GOD's image was its most important creature. But after the work of these men, our solar system, the earth and particularly man were reduced to insignificant specks. Thus, it seems that man not only lost his glory but also his very significance. However, this is looking from the inside out. With our current understanding of size and age of the universe, we should be looking from the outside in. It took GOD ten or so billion years just to make the nebular cloud necessary for the formation of our sun and solar system and it took five or so billion years to produce our current conditions. You now see how much GOD has done so far for mankind. Currently man is GOD'S most significant work. It looks like the Church got it right in the first place; however, they got it right for all the wrong reasons.

It has been said that the Dark Ages will end when philosophy comes down from the eternal and deals with the affairs of mankind. Well it was not intended, but the results of the above work seems to have done that. Lets hope that Partners with GOD for Mercy will be the start of a philosophical renaissance.

# More About the Author

---

## One of the Innumerable Stories
## that Generally Remains Untold

(Primarily for my Children and Grandchildren)

*July 2002*

# PREFACE

Some of the names and dates may have been changed.  This was not done to protect the innocent.  It was done to coincide with my memory.

I was born in Ft. Smith, Arkansas on the 27th day of April 1929, and just 7 months before the historic stock market crash. My Mother was Emma Lee Stanley Roberts and my Father was Thomas Lawrence Roberts. I was named Thomas George Roberts. The name George was after Senator George, the Senator from Georgia. I was not a junior because my Father had been previously married and had a son who was a junior. My Father had this son before my Mother was born. I had a half-brother who was older than my Mother. My Grandmother, Eva Self Stanley, on my Mother's side had a girl, Sarah Earlene Stanley, who was about one year older than I, a girl, Susie Mae Stanley, who was four months younger that I, and a boy, Phillip Evans Stanley, who was 4 years younger than I. My Grandfather on my mother's side, Grover Baxter Stanley, was younger than my Father and I can remember Daddy calling him "Young Feller" (fellow). I know a little about my mother's siblings, there were twelve of them and even less about her parents. I really know nothing about my Father's family.

Shortly after my birth, we moved to Drumwright, Oklahoma, where my Father had been offered a better paying job. I believe that Daddy was already in the laundry business by that time. The stock market crashed, Daddy lost his job, could not find work, and decided to return to Tifton, GA where Mother's relatives lived. The trip from Drumwright to Tifton was made in the only car (a 1923 Model T Coupe) that my parents were ever able to afford. A little before they reached Tifton, they ran out of both gas and money. They coasted into a country store that sold gas. The weather was already cold and Daddy had a nice leather jacket. He went into the store. After a short while, he returned and filled the car with gas. He went back into the store, and then returned with some food, but without his jacket. Once they reached Tifton, they moved in with my Grandparents. Those who could find work had to help take care of the others; Daddy sold the car in order to help carry the load. My Daddy and my Granddaddy, Baxter would go wherever work could be found. They would live together as cheaply as possible and send as much as they could back to Tifton. I believe the places he went to find work included Chicago, Illinois and Atlanta, Georgia. Daddy found a job in Atlanta that paid enough for him to send for Mother and me. My Brother, Russell was born in Atlanta on 15 October 1930. In late 1931, Daddy found a fairly good job in Savannah, Georgia, which was closer to home. We moved to Savannah and lived in a boarding house until we found a place on Lincoln Street, about three short blocks from Broghton Street, which is Savannah's main street. Here we lived in the downstairs part of a two-story house. The downstairs part was like an above the ground basement. My second brother, Hershell Lawrence Roberts, was born here on 29 May 1932. By the way, Russell's real name is Everett Neal Robert, but I was grown before I learned this. Mother wanted to name him Russell after Senator Russell the Junior Senator from Georgia. Later you will see that she named my third brother after Franklin D. Roosevelt, the President at that time.

The house on Lincoln Street was also about six or seven short blocks from Star Laundry, where Daddy worked. It was necessary to live near where Daddy worked; there was no extra money to pay for transportation. This place on Lincoln Street was becoming too small. We moved to a place at 514 East State Street. This place was part of a large brick building not unlike the row houses found in Baltimore, Maryland. There was a sidewalk that separated the wall of the building from the street. Our doorsteps came down from the floor level to the sidewalk. There were three or four steps and then you stepped onto the sidewalk. There were upstairs apartments, but they had separate steps. My first and only sister, Virginia Ruth Roberts, was born here on 15 September 1933. Mother did not want any girl babies and when Virginia was first carried to her in the hospital, she did not want to take her. Of course, this did not last and mother loved Virginia at least as much if not more than any of the rest of us. We don't really know why mother did not want any girls, but she did not tell any of us about her illegitimate child until a year or so before her death at the end of 1991. Mother developed a reputation for telling the truth that matched that of George Washington. In fact, she was better than George was; he could not tell a lie, Mother could, but would not. She went out of her way to tell the truth; even if hurt or offended someone and it would have been better left unsaid. None of Mother's people ever told us about her son who was named Aubrey James Roberts. Aubrey was born in Tifton and he was sired by one of the Roberts', of Tifton who don't seem to have been a relative of my father. Daddy knew of Aubrey when he married Mother in about 1927. Aubrey was born with a defect that had something to do with the size of his head.  This defect led to his death while he was still a toddler.  We have one photograph of Aubrey while being held by his Grandmother.  I believe that this is also the only photograph that we have of Grandmother.  She looks much like my Mother and Aunt Sue did when they were young.  When Mother told me about Aubrey, she said "I guess I was destined to be a Roberts."  It may have been that Mother's passion for telling the truth resulted from her having lived with a lie of omission since Aubrey's birth and it may also account for her not wanting any girl children.  The double standard was not only very strong in her time, but it was also accepted by both sexes.  Even other women looked down on the girl who made a "mistake", but not on the boy that contributed to the "mistake".

We moved from 514 East State Street to 518 East State Street.  A move of only two houses however our new house, which was only new to us, was a one-story frame house that at the time had been painted white.  It was also only one house from the corner of State Street and Houston Street.  The corner House was occupied by a retired sea captain who was a recluse and was believed to have a king's ransom hidden in his house that was locked at all times and he was never known to leave the house.  Mother would fix a tray and take him lunch from time to time.  After sometime, he would leave 50 to 70 cents on the tray when it was returned.  Twenty-five cents would buy four pounds of dressed fish (Crocker).  When this man died, the police barricaded his house, search it to the extent of breaking into the walls and taking up part of the floors.  After about a week or so, everything of value was hauled away, and the barricade removed.  This occurred around 10 O'clock in the morning.  When they left, the children entered the house to search for anything that might have been missed.  I found a corn plaster box that had $75 hidden in it.  This was a small fortune.  Daddy was making about $15 a week which was considered quite good for that time.  After Daddy convinced Mother, that to give this money to the police would be like dropping it in a black hole, she decided to keep it.  It wasn't long after this time that we moved to the 600 block of Congress Street, about two blocks closer to the Star Laundry.  This house must have been larger, because it surely was not nicer.  As I recall, it seemed to have not been painted, or maybe it was in need of being painted.

We did not live on Congress Street very long before we moved to 114 Houston Street, about 100 yards from where we lived on State Street.  This house was also a frame house, but it was much nicer and it had good paint. It was here that my third brother, David Franklin Roberts was born on 17 September 1937.  By this time, I was 8 years old and in the third grade at Chatham Elementary School.  This school was close enough that I could walk to school and back.  As I mentioned, David was named after the President.  However, his birth certificate was first filed by a nurse who took a liking to him and named him Odell Devon Roberts.  This had to be changed. There are also about four errors on my birth certificate that required affidavits to correct them.  These errors included the spelling of my first name and the statement that I was the fourth child born to my mother, and two of us were now living.  I can account for only two of these.  It is said that Daddy got drunk when I was born and that he was still drunk when he filled out my birth certificate.  Maybe the other children were from his previous life.

When David was born I was about 8 ½ years old.  My formal education began here on Houston Street.  I went to kindergarten at a Montessori School located on Houston Street across the square and south of our house. The kindergarten was close enough that Mother could watch me walk to school and to walk home.  I started 1st grade at Abercorn Street School, but before or by the time, I was supposed to have finished the first grade, the school was condemned and closed.  I was transferred to a school building that had been called Chatham Academy, but was changed to Chatham Elementary and Junior High School.  For some reason, I repeated all or part of the first grade.  Maybe I did not know my colors, but I did know how to do long division and this did not seem to please my teacher who was trying to teach the class to add.  The most terrifying and significant events that occurred during our stay on Houston Street where David's whole body was sunburned, the breaking of my left arm in four places – twice, Vera Jones, the period when the Star Laundry was closed, and the time when Mother's relatives had to stay with us.  David was left sleeping in his playpen which, was set up on the sidewalk near our front steps.  It was a hot day, the sun was bright, and Mother got busy and forgot him. When Mother did get to David, he was very red all over, crying and hysterical. Mother came to him just in time. A little longer and he would have been damaged for life. He suffered greatly for a long time, but he finally recovered completely. I first broke my arm when I was hanging by my heels from the high-bar of the uneven parallel bars in Washington Square. The shoe came off my left foot and I tried to break my fall with my left hand. As a result of the fall, my arm was in a cast for weeks, then in a splint for a week or more, and finally in a sling for about a week. The next day I got into a fight with a boy named Willabee Harvey. I threw one punch, a left hook, which caused my arm to break again in the same four places. Vera Jones was a girl who lived in the row houses on State Street. She was about a year older than me, she had quite a few dolls, and while I was in the first grade she tried to teach Russell and me all about sex and its results. A new building was built for the Star Laundry on the southeast corner of East Broad Street and 35th Street. When it was completed, the laundry on Bay Street was closed while the equipment was being broken down, removed and reinstalled at 35th Street. This took quite a few weeks and Daddy was unemployed during the time. Work was hard to find; the unemployment lines were long. All of Daddy's life, if there were no jobs to be had, he made jobs. Jobs like going to peoples houses with a push cart, picking up their dirty laundry, bring it home, washing and drying it in our back yard, folding it and returning it clean; or pushing an ice cream cart through the better neighborhoods trying to make a few sales; or any other task no matter how menial, even those where he was turned down because he was a white man. When we lived on State Street, Grandmother died. She must have been the only thing that held that family together. Those that were left at home including Granddaddy left to live with the older girls who by now had families of their own. Between this time and the time that we moved into Garden Homes in late 1940 or early 1941, Granddaddy, Ralph, Shelton, Earlene, Sue and Phillip stayed with us from time to time, but not all at the same time. Life was hard enough without having to share, but having temporary older "brothers", and a sister near my age, "Aunt Sue" to play with was a real joy. I don't remember Daddy ever treating those children any different than his own. To us children, it wasn't sharing; it was simply getting by together.  I can only remember seeing Phil once and I don't remember him staying long that time.

We moved when the Star Laundry opened on 35th Street.  We found a place at 535 East 35th Street.  It was less than a hundred yards from our house to Daddy's work station in the back of the Laundry where the clothes were brought in and all of the very large washing machines were lined up from one side of the laundry to the other.  Daddy was in charge of this section.  It seems to me that most of the men who worked for him were black and they called him Captain Tom.  At Christmas, Daddy would give each of them a fifth of whiskey.  One of the blacks would always say, after he took his first drink, "Captain Tom's whiskey is always just right.  If it had been any better, he wouldn't have given it to me, and if it had been any worse, I couldn't drink it."  Daddy did not buy this whiskey with his money, but the men were allowed to think that he did.  When school was not open Russell or I got to carry Daddy's lunch to him.  Lunch was called dinner and what we now call dinner was supper.  The first time that we showed up with lunch, Daddy would take us to each section in the laundry and explain their job to us.  He would introduce us in a way that was embarrassing to us, and funny to everyone else.  The three things that I remember most about living on 35th Street in addition to the above were the railroad, Sue's one lesson on sex education, and Jacquelyn (Jackie) Tolbert.  I attended school at 37th Street Elementary.  It was about four blocks from our house, but I was able to walk both ways and this was uneventful.

The railroad ran behind our house and the locomotives were steam engines that burned coal.  In the evening, the firemen would "accidentally" let a fair amount of coal fall from the coal car onto our side of the track.  Most of the children in the area would run along the track collecting this coal.  It was used for heating and cooking.  To preserve food for a while we had an ice box.  We did not know what a refrigerator was except, in factories where they made ice or ice cream.  Each day an ice truck would drive through the streets selling ice the way ice cream was sold a few years later.  We could buy a block of ice (12½ or 25 pounds, I don't remember which) for five cents.  We needed at least two blocks especially if we were going to have tea.  Tea was one of our biggest treats.

Sue like Vera Jones thought that Russell and I needed to know more about sex and that we would learn best by participating in a demonstration. The demonstration was not very successful as far as I was concerned. Russell seemed to be a better student. This only happened once and no one else ever learned of it. That is until now.

Jackie Tolbert was my first true love. There was a junkyard on East Broad Street. There was a place that made wrought iron for banisters, railings, windows, fences and other uses. There were also other kinds of light industries located on East Broad Street. I had or made a wagon that I used to collect scrap metals. When I got enough to sell, I would pull it to the junkyard and sell it by the pound. This was only one of the ways that I was able to make a little money. I may have picked this up from my daddy because I continued this kind of thing until extra money was no longer a problem. The point of this story is that I had saved a little money to buy something that I thought I really wanted. However, instead of buying what I had worked for, I saw a box of candy that looked to me as if it had been made for Jackie. When I gave the box, unwrapped, to Jackie she was very happy and I felt so good that I thought this must be what love is all about. I had never felt this good about anything that I had done before. As a result of this experience, I have and still do buy things and do things for people especially people that I love, when I see the need or see something that seems to have been made for them. I have not and I still don't like to buy presents just because someone thinks it should be done on certain days. There have been times when this has made me seem insensitive or thoughtless and has gotten me into some trouble. However, I don't believe that anyone that I have "hurt" this way has ever questioned my love. They just disapprove of my not being willing to follow the herd. I have found a compromise. On days that were considered as being gift giving days, I give money so they can get something that they really wanted.

We next moved to a place on 36th Street Court, which was just a short extension of 36th Street across Habersham Street. The extension was about 50 yards to the termination of 36th Street. We only lived there for a little more than a year. However, it seems that many things happened during this time. The schoolyard was across the alley from our backyard, which was fenced in.  There was a small store on the corner of the alley and Habersham Street. There were small, usually dirt road beds that separated the houses or stores on one street, say 36th Street, from those on say 37th Street.  In Savannah, we called these alleys, lanes.  My first job was at this store.  I delivered small grocery orders to houses within a few blocks of the store.  I walked and hand-carried the packages.  My pay was $2.00 a week and I worked during the summer.  I was saving to buy a used, but good, bicycle.  One day while I was working, a hurricane hit Savannah.  It blew down trees, power lines, signs, and other weak structures.  I delivered several orders during the storm. When walking into the wind, I could not fall down and making headway was slow.  Walking the other way, I had to watch my footing to keep from falling down and I had to avoid blown down trees and other debris.  Storms like this were really dangerous near the beach, but in Savannah, which is protected by a 60-foot bluff, the storms were not so dangerous.  In addition to the wind, our greatest danger was from flooding, due to inadequate drainage. There was a large tree; I believe that it was a China Berry Tree, next to our house.  Uncle Ralph kept his car parked near this tree, probably for shade. This same storm blew this tree over Ralph's car.  A large limb kept the trunk from reaching Ralph's car.  The trunk stopped about 2 inches short of the top of the car and the limb was not touching it on the other side.  The back and the front were covered with leaves and small branches.  Ralph was not home at the time.  He may have been at work with the Civilian Conservation Corps (CCC).  Uncle Shelton cut the branches away and backed the car out. It was unhurt, except for a few scratches.  At this time we didn't know what automobile insurance was, much less have any.  Shortly after this storm, I had saved enough money to buy my bicycle, so I quit work to enjoy my ac-complishment.  There were better bicycles, but I had the one I wanted.  I was both successful and happy.  Success is getting what you want and happi-ness is wanting what you have.

The biggest event during this time was the birth of my fourth and last brother, John Osborn Roberts who was born on 29 June 1940.  Mother was only 34, but she must have had an unusually bad time with Johnny.  She needed at least six weeks to recover enough to take care of us children.  The City Health Department made arrangements for all of us children, including my Aunt Sue, to spend six weeks at the Fresh Air Home at Tybee Island. This was as much a vacation for us as it was for Mother. Some of us had stayed at the Fresh Air Home the last two years, but our stay was for only one or two weeks. The Fresh Air Home is a charitable place. That is only poor people get to go there and none of them have to pay. This was the best summer that I ever had in Savannah. Several times, when I was in Savannah, I have thought about going to the Fresh Air Home to see if they are still doing such good work. If so, I would like to leave them something in my will. I still intend to do that.

I found that I could buy 100 biddies (baby chickens) for three dollars, 3 cents per bird. I bought 100, intending to raise them in my back yard until they were frying size, then I was going to try to sell them and make a huge profit. At the time, I did not fully understand the cost of the needed food, the equipment needed to feed and keep them watered, the time required, and I had no idea of how to go about selling them. My business plan consisted of a beginning and an end. The middle was to be improvised. I lost one bird to a cat and four or five to the battle for survival. When the rest reached frying size, there was no time to try to sell them. We had applied for a place in the new government housing project. Our application was accepted and we had to move quickly. No pets were allowed in the project much less chickens. Somehow the adults along with Sue's help, managed to cook these birds, both in the kitchen and in the back yard. They then stripped the meat from the bones and canned it in glass jars. The birds moved to the project with us.

One nearly tragic and one humorous incident occurred after our return from the Fresh Air Home, the humorous one first. When Hershell was in the third grade, he was sent home with a note that said "Hershell will not be allowed back in school unless he is wearing long pants." It seems that Hershell's manhood was too long for short-legged pants. Daddy would tell people that on the average his boys had the proper length "manhood", but Hershell got most of it. Maybe daddy was right, at least by comparison with Hershell the rest of us were lacking. The near tragic accident occurred when Russell's kite got tangled in some electric wires that ran between telephone poles. I don't know why, but all of the poles were called telephone poles and all of the wires were called electric wires. The kite was in wires that ran near the roof of a garage or garage apartment. Russell thought that he could reach the kite from this roof. When he tried, he lost his hold and fell. When he landed, his head hit hard. I thought that Russell might have been killed, but before anyone could get to him, he jumped up and said I am all right; I have got to go home. He took off running. Russell was suffering from some kind of concussion. When he got home, he barricaded himself in the kitchen, opened the icebox and would throw things; especially eggs at anyone that tried to reach him. Uncle Shelton finally reached him and calmed him down. I don't believe that Russell had any lasting effects from this accident, but I was very surprised that he was not seriously injured. Daddy and some of the others continued to tease him by saying that he hadn't been the same since.

We moved to Garden Homes in early 1941. These buildings were made of concrete blocks on a concrete slab and they had a red brick veneer. The inside walls were covered with plaster and painted white. They were new, clean, and beautiful and at first, bug free. We had a small yard in the back and front. Our front yard was divided by a small walk from our porch to the street. We acquired a rotary-type push-mower and it was a pleasure to have grass to cut. The backyard had a permanent clothesline (as yet there were no washers and dryers except in the laundries). In the center of each backyard there were under-ground garbage holes. Each hole contained a can and was covered with a hinged top; the garbage men would remove, empty, and replace these cans. We had three bedrooms upstairs and a bathroom. I don't remember anyone having showers. Downstairs there were two rooms and a fairly large closet beneath the stairs. There was a living room and a dining room, kitchen combination. These two rooms were connected by a large (more than twice the size of a door) pass-through. To us this was really moving up. The blacks soon had a similar project, just west of downtown. All of us, blacks and whites, when we moved in, said "praise be to God (Roosevelt)". Conditions were getting noticeably better and the economy really improved once the war involved the U. S. as a participant. Soon Henry J. Kaiser was building liberty ships in Savannah. Daddy left the laundry and became a ship fitter – whatever that is.  There was more to eat and at least the children had better clothes.

I may have gone to part of the 6th grade at a school on the corner of Waters Avenue and Anderson Street, but the first school that I remember attending after our move to Garden Homes was Chatham Jr. High School.  I was back in the building where I spent my first four grades.  I believe that it was near the end of the first year (7th grade) that I was arrested (picked up by a policeman) during class.  I was taken to the Police Station, which was near the school and questioned.

Near the end of the eighth grade when I was to complete junior high and move on to high school I learned that I had failed or failed to complete my geography requirements. (We did not graduate until we finished high school. Before that time, we just moved on or moved up.)  In order to move on to high school with my class, I had to make up this deficiency.  There was only about a month left before the school year ended.  I was sent to the Geography Teacher.  She gave me a textbook and told me to study a certain part of it for two weeks and then to return for a test to see if I could be given credit for this requirement or if I would have to attend summer school.  Summer School was something that I did not want to do.  I studied hard which was something that I could do, but did only when it was necessary.  I only studied to be able to pass a test, not just to learn something.  When I returned to the teacher to take my test, paper and pencil in hand, she asked me only one question – What are the ABC Countries of South America?  This question was so unexpected that my mind almost went blank.  After some moments, I came to my senses and answered – Argentina, Brazil and Chili.  She said fine, enjoy high school.  I believe that it was at this time that I realized that to make a good grade you should learn what the teacher wanted you to answer on the test and not necessarily what the subject being studied was really about.  You should think about what the teacher says and accept it.  Don't let your mind question it.

It was time for me to move on to high school, but which high school?  Savannah, at this time, had two public high schools, one was called Savannah High or Academic High, and the other was called Commercial High.  Commercial was something of a half-breed; it was a cross between a high school and a trade school. They dropped courses like algebra, trigonometry, physics and chemistry. They substituted courses like sales, bookkeeping, business law, typing, office practices and business math. Actually junior high was part trade school. In junior high, I took courses like shop, where I learned the fundamentals of wood working, during this period, I made things like, what-not stands and other small pieces of furniture that my Mother still had in her house when she had to move to a nursing home. I also made the desk and bookcases that were used in my office at home and were the outstanding feature of the office of TECHNOCO, a company that I formed after retirement from Civil Service. Education seemed to have lost this valuable aspect – that of learning how to do things – but with the advent of computers maybe it is coming back. Enough Philosophy for now, let's get back to the reason for two different kinds of high schools. When time came to move up to the ninth grade, each student was allowed to choose which school he or she wanted to attend. We were advised to select Savannah High if there was even a slight chance that we might get to go to college. If there was essentially no chance of going to college, we were advised to select Commercial High. Commercial High not only trained one for a job in commerce; they also had a placement service that helped you to find a job locally after graduation.

I chose Commercial High. Mother went to school through the sixth grade before she had to quit and go to work. Daddy claimed that he had gone to school for three years. His attitude was that in three years, one should be able to learn to read, write, and do arithmetic; after this, one should be able to be on his own. It was time to start helping the family. Mother wanted all of her children to finish high school. Daddy wanted them to start work and begin to carry their own weight as soon as possible. As it turned out, I was the only one that stayed in school through graduation. After leaving the Navy, Russell received a high school diploma by passing the High School Graduate Education Development (GED) Test. I guess that you could say that it was two for Mother and four for Daddy. However, I went on and earned four college degrees, so on the average, it was Mother six and Daddy four. I was to education, as Hershell was to "Manhood". On the average we had the right amount, but I got most of it.

Through high school I was not a particularly good student. I studied enough to get by, but again, I must have failed some subject because I had to go to summer school and take one course before graduating in August 1948. This plus a new draft law for the Army kept me from getting a job in Savannah and led to my joining the new U. S. Air Force, but more about this later.

Compared with the past, life in Garden Homes was very good. The food that we had wasn't a lot better, but now there was plenty of it. The biggest event of the week used to be when mother came home from the Bargain Corner with the week's groceries. We would be waiting to help her bring them in to see if there were any goodies. But even when life is better, bad things happen. A terrible thing happened when Johnny was just old enough to walk well. He got some matches and went behind the hedge near our house. He was striking the matches and dropping them. One landed on his shoe and set the leg of his corduroy overalls on fire. Johnny started screaming. Daddy jumped the hedge ripped the clothes off Johnny, threw them on the ground, and was stomping them out. Johnny rolled back and fell onto a large ant-hill. His leg was not only burned from the ankle to near the hip on the outside and the ankle to near the crotch on the inside, but it was also covered with ants. As bad as this was and still is a problem for him, it was only one of Johnny's many serious problems.

The only time that I can remember being hurt by Mother was when she took money that I brought in to help the family and gave some of it to Russell so that he could buy feed for his racing pigeons. I told Mother that I was helping to pay for necessities and not to raise Russell's pigeons. Mother didn't feel this way. She told me that the feed was bought with her and daddy's money. She pointed out that they would not have let the pigeons do without food if I had not brought any money home. I tried to understand her point and not get my feelings hurt. I think that she tried to understand my side because if any thing like this happened again I did not learn of it. It seems that I always had or created a job. Among other things that I did was, I shined shoes, collected scrap metal, had a 136 customer morning (before school) paper route for about seven months, and I worked for the Savannah Theaters Company where I reached my life's pentacle of self-importance. Jim McKay, who lived directly behind our house, and I got a job at the Odin

Theater as ushers.  We both worked the night shift.  The users had to wear a uniform, and the head usher who was (so to speak) in charge of the shift, wore a fancier one, one with more frills.  There was in addition to other personnel, a manager and an assistant manager, who wore business suits.  To save money the Savannah Theaters Company decided to replace their Assistant Manager with a person who was called the Chief of Staff.  The Chief of Staff was to be hired from the student body of Armstrong College, a junior college located in Savannah.  The Chief of Staff was to report for duty after school was out, and work until closing.  During this time he assumed the duties of the Assistant Manager, which included overseeing the head usher, helping to check out the cashier and concessions each night and to accompany the Manager to the bank to make the night deposits.  He was also to be outside the theater, meeting people, being friendly, and promoting the movies that were being shown.  The Chief of Staff, like the Manager, wore a business suit.  The Manager of the Odin Theater told the front office that he would rather have me than any of the college students for his Chief of Staff.  I did not know that he had done this until they told him to go ahead and let me try to do the job.  When he offered the job to me, I could hardly believe it, but I was quick to say that I wanted to try to do a good job.  The next day I took part of the money that I had saved and bought myself a brown double-breasted business suit.  During my first workday between 7 PM and 9 PM, when I was strutting back and forth in front of the Odin Theater, in my new suite, I reached a peak of my sense of importance that has yet to be matched.

The public schools in Savannah allowed a student to fail a grade only once.  After repeating a grade, he was promoted automatically.  Herschell was sick a good part of his early years and he was promoted without learning how to read until there was no way that he could pass a course.  He spent his entire educational career in elementary school.  When he was old enough to be allowed to, he dropped out and tried to find a job.  He was a part of the available work force, but he could not read or write.  It turned out that there was nothing lacking in his ability to learn and when he became personally motivated, he learned to read and write.  More details about Herschell are included in the notes.  Johnny's problems caused him to wind up in the same situation as Herschell except that he convinced himself that he could not learn to read.  Johnny remained this way until sometime after his second marriage, when his wife, Kay was able to teach him.  The first thing that he wrote was a letter to me.  It is in my files.  I was so happy that I cried.  I called Johnny and after congratulating him, I said write your Mother a letter and do it now!

During the war everyone was encouraged to plant a victory garden.  This was just one of the ways that we showed our patriotism.  Waving flags and flying flags everywhere didn't amount to much; we all knew that we were in a battle for survival.  The farmer who owned the land just east of Garden Homes offered a plot of land, bordering his property to each family that was willing to work it and help keep the children from crossing over onto his land.  We had a garden for two or three years.  On my part, I grew watermelons, cantaloupes and cucumbers.  Until very recently this is as close as I ever came to knowing what it must be like to live in the country and produce ones own food.

Mother believed that it was not respectable for young unmarried women to work.  After they were married they should be too busy keeping the family, the foundation of society, to have time for work.  Virginia took this to heart and for nearly all of her life; she has been able to avoid jobs outside the home.  Since girls were not supposed to work, they had to help with all of the housework.  Mother felt that we boys should then have to contribute part of our earnings to Virginia.  This seemed right to me and I never had any trouble with it.  The money was given to Mother not Virginia.  That way it was spent mostly for needs.  Virginia had more than any of the boys.  It seemed that when Mother would buy something for one or more of us, she also bought Virginia something.

By 1947 when Daddy was 64 years old his arthritis was beginning to make work difficult, all of the children were old enough to help take care of each other, so mother went to work.  The best that she could do was to take a job housekeeping at St. Joseph's Hospital.  She kept this job until she was no longer physically able to work.  This happened when she was involved in an automobile accident; Johnny was driving the car.  This was a major turning point in Mother's life; from here on, her health was slowly downhill.

Two other things that might need to be mentioned here are organized sports and the continuation of my sex education. More details will be included in the notes. However the organized sports, except for my unsuccessful attempts at high school football and baseball, only amounted to our sandlot ballgames, somehow evolving into a type of semi-organized league. We did not have a schedule, as such, but we did manage to play most of the teams in the neighborhood at lease once. The sex lessons amounted to Vivian Harden taking on most of our scout troops in group educational sessions.

After graduating from high school, I was unable to get a job at any of the places suggested by the placement service. The problem was that if they hired me and then I was drafted, they would have to rehire me once I had completed my service-time, which was 22 months. They did not want to hire me, train me, then try to hire someone for the time that I was in the Army, and have to rehire me when I was discharged. They all told me, fulfill your service obligation and then we will hire you if we still need someone. We were required to register for the draft on certain days that were determined by our age and our birthday. Each day you could read in the newspaper who was supposed to register the next day. The registration office was in the downtown post office. When it was my day to register for the draft, I learned that the recruiting office for each of the services was also located in the post office and they were on the same floor. The recruiting officers walked up and down the halls trying to talk the men in the registration line to join their branch of the service. I think that they wanted to fill their quotas for the month in one day. Each would argue that it would be month's maybe even a year before you would be drafted and then you would have to go into the infantry. You could enlist now and maybe choose your job, a job that would keep you out of the infantry, let you see the world in the navy or maybe become a hero in the new U. S. Air Force. However, you had to enlist for three years, not 22 months. After more than an hour of waiting in line, I bought their argument. I dropped out of line and joined the Air Force.

In about another hour of filling out forms and taking some simple tests, I signed up and was sworn in. They gave me a train ticket through New Orleans to San Antonio, Texas; some meal tickets, and about three hours to get home, get my gear together get to the Central of Georgia Train Station, and be off to a new phase of my life. The one big trip by myself before this had been a 30-mile train ride to Guyton, GA where I spent the night and saw what real country folks were like. This trip must have been about 1700 miles to a land that I had only seen in the movies. I was on my own. Somehow I felt that I was, if not a man, at least I was an independent person. But, of course, I was now a dependent of my Uncle Sam instead of my Mother and I had been well trained to obey those upon whom you are dependent. Therefore, I never got into any real trouble while I was in the Air Force.

I spent 13 weeks in basic training at Lackland Air Force Base, San Antonio, Texas. While I was in basic training, I found two ways to make some extra money. I made $20 for participating in one boxing match, but my most lucrative activity was cleaning fatigues and hanging them out to dry for 25 cents each. I did this once a week for several weeks. I almost got in trouble for not eating everything on my plate one day at lunch. You could take all you wanted when you passed through the food line, but everyone at the table had to eat everything on their plate before anyone could leave the table. There was one squad at each table. I had some ham that looked to me as if it was spoiled. I refused to eat it. My squad had to sit at the table without saying a word. We sat there until it was time to start serving supper. I was put on report (gigged) and my squad was marched back to our barracks. That evening everyone in my barracks came down with food poisoning. They would try to make it to the latrine to throw up, but many did not make it. They threw up in the aisle between the bunk beds. Emergency clinics were set up in the latrines of most of the barracks near us. Everyone had to get in line to receive medication that made them throw up if they had not done so already. After throwing up for awhile they were given a medication to make them stop. They then returned to their beds and remained there. I did not have to take these medications and I did not have to report to the Office of our Company Commander who was a Captain. However, I was gigged fairly often. There was a small but annoying personality conflict between our Assistant Flight Marcher – a Corporal Burns, who was the only other person from Georgia that I met while in basic. In fact, I believe that I was the only one in my flight that was from Dixie. If I had been in the Army, my flight would have been called a platoon.  One of our past times was verbally re-fighting the civil war.  The Yanks were badly outnumbered and the south won again.  Because of this conflict and my nature of taking advantage of it whenever it would bring a laugh, I was gigged quite a few times, enough for me to get to know the Captain much better than the other recruits.  When basic was completed the well behaved got promoted to Private First Class (PFC) while others with much fewer gigs than I just went from Recruit to Private.  See the notes for more details about basic training.  The promotion to PFC was important because an increase in pay came with it and you got started on the right foot for your next promotion.  I believe that the pay of a Recruit was $75 per month, but it may have been $52.50 for my first month. A PFC's pay probably was about $77.50.  There was no thought of ever get-ting rich.  However, for the time and coming out of the South during the depression, I felt that I was doing fairly well because my pay also included food, clothing, housing, medical and travel expenses.  A single man could get by and still send a little money home.

After basic training, I was transferred and assigned to Carswell Air Force Base, Ft. Worth, Texas.  Carswell was the home of the Eighth Air Force Head-quarters, the 7th Bomb Wing, and across the flight line was a large division of Convair Corporation that made B36 bombers and they were also working on the XC99, a cargo plane.  The Bomber Squadrons or the 7th Bomb Wing flew B36's.  These planes were truly long-range bombers.  They had ten en-gines, six that drove props and four that were jets.  The jets were used for assistance on take-off when the plane was heavily loaded and for additional speed when the plane was over target.  For me, there was a lot of glamour associated with the 8th AF and Carswell AFB, but as you will see, very little if any of it rubbed off on me.

I arrived at Carswell ahead of my orders and reported to a transit com-pany for a few days until my orders arrived.  For the most part all I had to do was wait, but one day, I was sent to the stockade (jail) to pull guard duty. They gave me a rifle (loaded) and a three prisoner work detail to guard.  I was told that if I let anyone of them escape I would have to complete his sentence. Needless to say, none escaped.  When my orders arrive, I was assigned to the Headquarters and Headquarters Company of the 7th Bomb Wing.  The

Company then assigned me to work in the Base Security Office.  A Major was in charge and there were one and sometimes two Lieutenants.   There was a Tech Sergeant who was in charge of the enlisted personnel and there were two or three civilian female secretaries.  The work was clerical and my high school training probably led to my getting this assignment, if not it sure made learning and performing the work easier.  I enlisted for three years and wound up serving nearly four.  My move from Lackland AFB to Carswell AFB was my only permanent change of station.  My first job assignment was also my last.  The Korean War broke out and I was ready to do whatever I was assigned to do, but like everyone else, I never volunteered for anything. I became a veteran and qualified (earned) for the benefits of the Korean Bill of Rights while setting at my desk in Ft. Worth, Texas.  The Bill of Rights along with my choosing commercial high school and the re-start of the draft by President Truman which led to my joining the Air Force were the major events that determined the course of my life for now and for years to come.

It seems that what goes around comes around.  It is now more than 50 years since I started working in the Security Office and in a sense, I am back where I started.  The only company that I still have anything to do with is Science Applications International Corporation (SAIC).  The Security Manager for SAIC is Betty Roberts, my second and current wife.  It seems like I am again working for the Major.

During my years at Carswell, I went on two TDY trips, one to Tinker AFB in Oklahoma and one to Campbell AFB in Tennessee.  Campbell AFB is attached to, or is part of Camp Campbell, Kentucky, but it is on the south side and is actually in Tennessee.  Twice I also got to ride in Air Force planes while I was on leave or on a three-day pass.  You had to apply for the available space on these flights and wait your turn, but it did not cost you anything.  One of my flights was to Savannah and back to Carswell.

I tried to continue my education or improve myself during my off duty time.  I went to Texas Christian University's Night School and took a course in shorthand and I took a correspondence course in plane geometry.  I also had some on-base training courses.

When I was in basic, it was like being in the Army.  Someone was always in charge and we marched everywhere.  If we didn't have somewhere to go we just marched around.  We also did a lot of double-time and made force-marches.  We learned to shoot weapons and otherwise behave like a soldier.  When I left Lackland, I left these things there.  I don't believe that I marched more than once while at Carswell.  Life at Carswell was like living in a city.  You did not have to leave the Base, but of course, we did when we could afford it.  I went to Galveston Beach and to Little Laredo, Mexico among other places.  At Carswell, I had a home (barracks), a place to eat (mess-hall), a theater, a recreation center (USO Club), a social club (NCO Club), a sports complex where organized sports between the companies were held, a PX, etc. and free transportation between each place.  For the most part, life was like getting up and going to work five days a week and having the weekends free.  As part of the organized sports, I was a member of the two-hand touch football team for the HQ and HQ Squadron, 7th Bomb Wing.  I played for two years.  I was the center, who along with the two ends, was an eligible receiver.  We won the Base Championship and were undefeated both of the two years that I played.

After the Korean War was underway, President Truman extended the enlistment of all members of the services for one year.  I was pleased that it was not for the duration as it was during the Second World War.  However, for those who were about to be discharged in a few months and especially for those who were to be discharged the next day, this extension was quite upsetting.  One Airman wrote a letter of complaint to Truman.  He addressed it to "GOD Almighty", Washington, D.C.  We were told that the letter was delivered to Truman unopened.  If this is true, then God did not answer his prayers.  A wonderful thing that Truman did was to take what for me was the first step toward racial integration and it was a giant step for mankind in this country.  He by executive order, integrated the services.  Overnight blacks were assigned to the white companies and moved into the barracks and jobs with the whites.  There were no more black companies.  The Air Force along with the other services took their first step to becoming color-blind.  This step was made without riots, fanfare, or a thousand news analyst and "experts" explaining it in many ways and discussing all of its possible implications for the war and civilian life after the war.  The world seems to have been much simpler and yes better without an excessive media coverage that even attempts to replace and thereby interfere with our judicial systems. At first there were a few confrontations in some of the barracks, but they only involved a couple of individuals and were short lived. This integration move was made somewhat easier because they let the highest three grades (called the first three grades) of the enlisted ranks apply for and receive allowances (money) for quarters, and rations and live off the base. By this time I was a Staff Sergeant (S/SGT) which was the lowest of the first three grades. Two others of the first three grades in my company and I found a nice place to live off base and applied for quarters and ration allowances. These were granted and we made the move. From here on, life was like having a place in the city and a job on the base. My pay including allowances was just over $240 a month. I only had to pay one third of the rent and I had saved enough money to buy a used car, a 1942 Plymouth Business Coupe. At this time, I also got my first drivers license; I was twenty-two.

I did not consider my pay sufficient to support a wife and family and had so far not been in a relationship that involved sex. In fact, I had yet to be alone with a girl where such a relationship could get started, except for one brief time in Garden Homes when I was alone with Betty Sanderfer. Well nearly alone, she was baby-setting and because of the presence of the baby and my shyness or lack of maturity, things did not go too far. However, to tell the whole truth I did one day, with three other Airmen, visit a hotel in downtown Fort Worth where girls worked. These girls had sex for pay. Some men will sometimes do things as part of a group that they would never do by themselves. I don't know, but I also think that there are some men that will do things when they are by themselves, if they feel that they will not be caught or found out. I have fairly well managed to not be among this group.

It seems that I have skipped religious training, so let me try to catch up here before I leave the Air Force. My moral training began as soon as I could comprehend what my Mother was saying. Her training was not only vocal but was also by example and it was backed up by spankings when needed. Daddy, by example tried to undo Mother's good work, but his training was not backed up by punishments. Mother's training is the only one that had a lasting effect. Until I was 8 or 9 years old and living on Houston Street, no one in my family or any of Mother's relatives, as far as I know, had ever gone to church. There was a Baptist Church near our house. I became interested in the goings on there. I went in, and they showed me around, and invited me and my family to return the next week. The next week Mother cleaned me up and let me attend by myself. She had to stay home and take care of the others including David, who was a new baby. I went to Sunday school for a few weeks, before they wanted me to be baptized. I agreed and a date was set. But, before this date arrived, I had an accident that caused a fairly large cut under my chin and knocked me dizzy. The lady who was to become my God Mother and Guardian Angel (she has been dead for more than 30 years, but she is still on duty and is doing a super job) saw me fall. She had her chauffeur stop. They picked me up and put me in the back seat of her car with her – blood and all. They took me to her doctor, had me cleaned up, sewn up and examined for other injuries. She then took me home and invited me and my family, to come to her church the next Sunday. This lady was the wife of the Vice President of the Central of Georgia Railroad Company who was stationed in Savannah. She was a member of Christ Episcopal Church, one of the largest churches in Savannah. It was also the oldest active church in the nation. This was the church where John Wesley served when he first came to this country. Mother and I attended the next Sunday. We were very impressed with the church, but we were impressed with Mrs. Knapp even more. My family became members and remained so until I left to join the Air Force. Mother remained a member until her death. All of us except for Johnny were baptized at one time. I went through all of the training classes and attended the confirmation ceremony. I attended regularly and learned to help with the services (mass). I also was in the Choir for a while, but when they asked me to always sing very quietly, I got the message and quit. In my high school years, I began to attend less and less. After I joined the Air Force, I stopped going to church except for a few times to increase my chances of meeting girls. I guess that I figured that since I volunteered to join an organization whose purpose was to become more efficient at killing people, I didn't need to burden myself with constant reminders that this was sinful. I never have been able to comprehend the concept of killing people in God's name, by God's direction, or with God being on my side.  I did not attend church again until my children were old enough to need to go to Sunday school and even then my attendance was perfunctory and stopped once the children were about 12 years old.  Since then, the only times that I attended was for things like the christening of a grandchild.  However, I have read and thought of religions and Gods and I have written a paper (small book) on what God really is and why we exist and our justification for being here, our raison d'etre.  The paper is called Rambling Thoughts.  If you get to read this paper you will think more of or less of me, but in either case you will know my understanding of these things and what I really believe.

Getting back to my last days in the Air Force, by this time the fighting in Korea had stopped.  Truman allowed the service extensions to be reduced.  I was to be discharged in August instead of September.  I had been nominated for promotion to Tech Sergeant.  The promotion board essentially told me that they wanted to promote me, but not if I was going to leave the service next month.  I had decided to give civilian life a try, so I was not promoted, but I knew that I could reenlist anytime during the next six months at my grade of S/SGT if civilian life did not work out.  After being mustered out, I drove my car from Ft.Worth, TX to Savannah, Georgia.  Upon entering the city, I blew a spark plug out of the block.  The car started making a loud explosion like noise and attracted much attention, but I drove it home before I dared to cut it off.  I was never able to start the car again.  As soon as I decided to go to Armstrong Junior College and was accepted as a student, I sold the car "as is" for almost as much as I had paid for it.  I started civilian life on foot.

Compared to the work, to which I had become accustomed, the opportunities available at that time were more like manual labor, than a job.  It looked like it would be back in the Air Force if my paid for attempt at college education failed.  In high school I was not prepared for college work and I had doubts about being able to catch up, while trying to keep up.  Even though for a college student, I had gone to the wrong high school and had not been a good student, these doubts were unfounded.  Notice that I had doubts about being able to pass not fears of failing.  If I had tried and not been able to make good grades and had to drop out I felt that I would be proud that I had made the effort and not ashamed that I had not succeeded.

Armstrong Junior College was a two-year school that offered an Associate Degree in Arts (A.A.). I entered school as a freshman in September of 1952. Nine months later in June of 1953, I graduated without ever having been a sophomore and I was one of two students that had an "A" average. I had either the highest or 2nd highest average. I was able to accomplish this by taking the college level GED test when it was offered to me during my first quarter. I made good grades on the test and received enough freshmen and sophomore credits so that by the end of my first nine months, I could meet all of the requirements for the A.A degree except for one course. I noticed that this course was being given in Armstrong's night school. During the second quarter, I carried a full load in the day school and enrolled in the night school to take the needed course. Early in my third quarter I requested that I be allowed to graduate in June. At first they objected, but after checking against the requirements in their catalog, they agreed to let me graduate in June. To prevent this from happening again they prohibited a student from taking courses in both the day and night schools at the same time.

I was now a good student with good grades and held an A.A. Degree from an accredited college. The state schools had to admit me, but as I found out they did not have to do it without conditions. For one thing they did not have to accept the GED test results. At Armstrong, I was living at home, but at one of the state universities, I would have to pay for my room and board. The $110 that I received from the Government for being a Korean War veteran was not quite enough and eventually, I would need some kind of car. The best job that I could quickly get was one of manual labor at the Union Bag and Paper Company (now called Union Camp). I started at $1.35 per hour, but due to the union, in a couple of weeks I got a raise to $1.45 per hour. This caused me to have a little trouble with the union, but I convinced them that I was only going to work for a few months so they stopped pressuring me to join the union and pay dues. After working for about four months I had saved enough money to accept admission to the University of Georgia. They admitted me as a junior, but they did not give me credit for two years of English, based on the GED test. It was left up to each department to decide to accept or not accept the GED test.  Only the English Department refused to accept them.  This meant that I was short twenty-quarter hours of work. By staying at school for seven consecutive quarters and taking one course by correspondence (this was a tough way for me to take a course), I was able to complete the requirements for a B.S. Degree with a major in Physics and graduated with an A average.  I was also elected to Phi Beta Kappa, Phi Kappa Phi, Sigma Pi Sigma and Pi Mu Epsilon honor societies.

It was now August of 1955 but I would not be able to attend the graduation ceremony and pick up my certificates until June of 1956.  It had been almost three years since I left the Air Force and I had earned two degrees with a major in the field of physics, which was offering the highest starting salaries for college grads.  When I started college I was hoping that I could get a job that paid $5,200. a year – one hundred dollars a week!  This was about twice what I was making at the Paper Company.  After graduation I only interviewed with two companies – Bell Labs and Westinghouse Beatis Plant in Pittsburgh.  They each paid expenses for a visit to their facility.  I was offered $6,800.  I thought that if education was worth this much, I ought to get a little more of it so I stayed at Georgia to try to get a Masters Degree in Physics.  I could have gone to another school.  I still had about two years left on my GI Bill benefits and schools were paying for good students especially good students in physics.  Georgia offered me the Alumni Foundation Fellowship.  This fellowship required no services and paid me $1,500 for attending GA for one academic year.  That is a little over $150 per month tax tree.  This gave me $260 plus tuition and fees, all tax-free and I had time to tutor for the Athletic Department, which paid quite well.  I must have treated the money from tutoring as tax free also, because up to this time, I don't remember having yet filled out an income tax return form, even though income taxes were withheld from my military pay during at least my last years of service.  Being paid to go to school seemed to be too good to be true. Why face the unknown when you can be well paid to stay with the known? I was now a graduate student at the UGA.  I started the fall quarter of 1955 and began the experimental work for my thesis project.  In addition to this work, I took only ten hours of class work per quarter except for the summer quarter when I attended only one class.  My Major Professor was Tom Barr who left UGA after my first quarter.  He took a civil service job at Redstone Arsenal.  He agreed to review my thesis if I would bring it to Huntsville.  I agreed and under these conditions I was allowed to continue the experimental work without the daily supervision of a major professor.  This worked out well and proved to be good training, because I had to do my Ph.D. research with much less supervision.  In fact, I had to do many of the things that a major professor gets done before the Ph.D. candidate begins his work.  Just for the record my master's thesis was titled "The Adsorption of gases on Porous Copper and Porous Silver Plates."  This work was hoped to be a help to the Oak Ridge National Laboratory where uranium isotopes are separated through the technique of gas diffusion of uranium containing compounds.

UGA did not yet have a Ph.D. program in Physics and very few of the Southeastern Universities had one.  UGA at this time was expanding their master's program in preparation for offering a Ph.D. Degree and a few years after I left they did offer one.  Due to this expansion program, I may have received somewhat better training than had been previously offered.  Since the master's degree at UGA was a terminal degree as the A.A. Degree was at Armstrong, I would have to look to another school if I wanted to pursue a Ph.D. Degree instead of taking a job.  I finished my thesis and my class requirements at the end of the summer quarter in 1956.  My UGA transcript shows that I had now earned the Master's Degree and was graduated, but again I would have to wait until June of 1957 to pick up my certificate, and again I had an "A" average and I was elected to the Society of the Sigma Xi.  Sigma Xi is an honor society for graduate students that are judged to have performed a good research project and produced a good report.  Only a few students were elected.  I had now earned three degrees in a little less than four years and I had also been out of school working for money to help pay for my education for several months during this time. At no time during this period did I feel that I was in a hurry.  I was not trying to accomplish anything out of the ordinary and never thought about setting records. I just took advantage of every opportunity offered, completed it, and looked to what was needed to be done next.  There was no master plan.  I was only trying to learn.  I was not preparing to be a doctor, lawyer, engineer, Indian Chief or physicist.  In fact when I started, I did not know that a physicist existed.

I was a third quarter junior before the veterans administration forced me to pick a major.  When they did, I picked physics because it seemed easy at the time and I was doing quite well in my physics classes.  I think that my choice was also influenced by the fact that all of the students considered this to be the toughest row to hoe.  To study physics and still carry a good average was like receiving double recognition.

I decided that I would continue my education and try to get a Ph.D. Degree.  It was too late to compete for fellowships and assistantships for the school year starting in the fall quarter of 1956, so I accepted a position of Instructor of Physics at UGA.   I lectured to students taking their first and only science course.  These students were education majors and others who had a requirement of a science class for graduation.  This was the type of work that none of the professors wanted to do.  I did it for three-quarters and found it to be fun.  During this year I applied to several schools for admission to their Ph.D. program and for financial help.  All of these schools except one (University of Miami, which did not have a Ph.D. program) accepted me and offered some help.  The best offers came from the University of Virginia and Duke University.  I visited both schools and liked Duke best, but for financial reasons, I decided to attend University of Virginia.  The head of the Physics Department was an internationally famous physicist, Jessie W. Beams.  Professor Beams had visited UGA while I was working on my master's experiment.  He inspected my work, showed interest in it, and was pleased that I seemed to be doing it unsupervised.  I believe that his visit had influence on my being offered UVA's best fellowship.  I was offered their special fellowship, which paid $2500 and required no duties.  These fellowships were used to attract those considered to be the most outstanding students.  I was very honored and really surprised.  Speaking of honors, at UGA I was given (won) the Wheatley Physics Award.  This award was presented to the most outstanding physics student.  It is not offered every year to the best physics student.  It is offered only when the selection committee thinks the best student is also outstanding.  This was my highest educational honor and it carried an honorarium of $500 or $1,000, I don't remember which.  It would have been nice to also have received a metal, certificate, or something like that.  However, years later, my oldest nephew, Dave Roberts, visited UGA to be considered for a football grant-in-aid. During this trip, he was taken on a tour of the campus, which included a visit to the Physics Building. This is a building that was only in the planning or dreaming stages when I was a student. Dave said that when he walked into the lobby, he saw a bronze plaque that listed the winners of the Wheatley Physics Awards; he told the guide "hey look, there is my uncle's name". I have never seen this plaque but it is better than a metal.

I was scheduled to enter UVA for the fall quarter of 1957. While I was an instructor, Tom Barr had me apply for a summer job at his Lab at Redstone Arsenal. I did and I was offered a 90-day appointment at the grade of GS-9. I accepted and spent the summer of 1957 in Huntsville. I rented a room in a nice old lady's house for the summer. This was my first experience of working in a fairly large government laboratory. This laboratory was just a collection of several smaller labs that consisted of four to six people each. Each small lab was working on somewhat different projects. My lab was starting to look into plasma physics; a fairly new field and very few univer-sities at this time were investigating plasmas and plasma phenomenon. I enjoyed my job and the people that I worked with, but when fall came I was ready to go to UVA.

Before I completed the first phase of my formal education, I need to up-date the events that have occurred concerning the opposite sex (my love life). For most of the time in school, I was too busy and too poor to have time for or to afford a girl. During this period I did not own a car and I lived in a dorm, also, I was something of a workaholic and all of this made establishing a close relationship difficult. However there was a girl a few years younger than I, who was a graduate student in chemistry. We made contact during activities where science students came together, and we kind of paired up. Her name was Anne Harbin. She had been a good undergraduate student who also advanced fairly rapidly. She earned her BS degree in education before I entered college in 1952 and took a job teaching in Atlanta, which was her hometown. She had returned to UGA to try to earn an MS Degree in chemistry. She lived in a women's dorm that had a fairly early curfew, even for graduate students. We became fairly good friends and remained that way until after my thesis was typed, corrected, accepted by my graduate committee, and turned in for publication. About the middle of my last year as a student at UGA Anne had found an apartment and moved out of the dorm. Her apartment had once been the attic of a family's house. It was converted to an apartment and a private entrance was added, so that she could come and go without bothering the family downstairs. Here Anne typed all of the drafts and final version of my thesis. To do this we spent time working together and becoming more familiar with each other. The night that my thesis was completed and ready to be turned in, our familiarity almost became complete. We were close to becoming consenting adults. A couple of dates later, when I had completed my orals and the defense of my thesis which was the only time that I missed Tom Barr not being present at UGA, we both consented and continued consenting when conditions permitted.

This situation continued until June of 1957 when we both picked up our MS Degrees and I was off to work at Redstone Arsenal, planning to enter UVA in the fall. UVA had been and was still a boy's school, but had recently allowed girls to enter the graduate school and I did not know this. I thought that this meant a possible permanent separation for Anne and I. I could not understand why she was taking it so well. I knew that it takes a lot of love to make a marriage work and that Anne had enough for both of us. She knew that I was not ready for marriage. I thought that she was facing a year or more separation too well. I understood it when I arrived at UVA and Anne was there. She had applied for and had been accepted for work toward a Ph.D. in chemistry and she even had an assistantship. Our situation was now the same as it was at UGA except that we were both living in dorms. I stayed in the dorm for the year, but Anne and two other girls were able to rent a house for what they were paying to stay in the dorm. There were only two bedrooms in the house and Anne shared one with a girl named Carolyn. To me this was just a smaller dorm, except that there were no curfews, and boy friends could come and go as the girls allowed, but they could not stay nor use the bedrooms. Anne and I dated as time and workloads permitted.

My year at UVA was by my standards, not good. My grades had been fair but not great. The chances that I would get a thesis project that I wanted looked like it might take years – more details in the notes. I was feeling discouraged and disappointed in myself. However, none of my problems had anything to do with Anne. In fact, she had been a positive factor, maybe the only one. I had been offered another 90-day appointment at Tom Barr's Lab at Redstone Arsenal and this at the grade of GS-11, which paid very well for these times. I went back to Redstone not knowing what to do the next year and Anne returned to Atlanta. We both tentatively assumed that we would be back at UVA the next fall. At Redstone, the more I thought about UVA the less I wanted to go back and the more I missed Anne. Once you become accustomed to a good thing, it becomes difficult to do without. Anne made two trips from Atlanta to see me. On the second trip I decided to stay at Redstone where I was excited about my work and to marry Anne. At this time Anne was not fond of Huntsville, but to get married, she would move anywhere. After this decision was made, UVA offered me another fellowship. This surprised me. If I had been the selection committee, I would have made better use of the fellowship. I would have given it to one of the many others who were more deserving. I could not consider accepting the fellowship knowing that I could not give 100 percent to UVA. I had made a clean break and it would remain that way forever. I am proud of the honors UVA had paid me and I am very disappointed that I let them down, but now it was time to make my education pay by doing a good job at Redstone.

I went to Atlanta and married Anne. We had everything a church wedding had, including elaborate dresses for the bride, and bridal party, except that the wedding was held in her parent's house. What we didn't have was money for a honeymoon. There were wedding rings, but there was no engagement ring. The money that I had was spent to fix the brake system on my car after it caught on fire during my drive to Atlanta to get married. I had enough left for one night in a motel just outside Atlanta and our trip back to Huntsville. That was our honeymoon. The wedding was on November 14, 1958. Prior to the wedding, I had used a feature of my veteran's benefits that was about to expire to acquire a loan to buy a lot and have a house built. I had been living in one half of a duplex with Charles Cason who owned the duplex. Since my new house was not yet under construction, Charles moved in with his parents who also lived in Huntsville and Anne moved in with me. We stayed in the duplex for a number of months until our home at 2712 Mastin Lake Road was ready for occupancy. We lived here until

August 1972, when we moved to 2815 Bentley Street. The house on Mastin Lake Road had about 1300 square feet, with no garage, and was becoming too small for our family. The house on Bentley had 3600 square feet and a large single car garage. We lived here until Anne died in December 1994. I owned the house for about two years more.

My status with the Civil Service changed in September 1958 from a 90-day appointment to a career conditional appointment. I was now a permanent employee that is a career employee, but my job was conditional. This was like having an academic appointment without tenure. This trial period lasted for three years. Anytime during this period I could have been released (fired without cause). After three years, they either had to let you go or give you a career appointment. This was like having tenure and it was very difficult for a boss to have one of his career employees fired. In one respect, I was different from all of the other civil servants except those who also held a research position, - a man in the job position. That is, there was only one man in each job and in the event of a reduction in force, no one else could qualify for your job and claim it because they had more seniority. However, if the job was eliminated, you were gone; there was no one anywhere for you to bump. My name was the only one that ever appeared on my register.

We were doing basic research; I loved it, and planned to spend my life doing basic research. However, things evolved and my job changed slowly to the point where I was spending less time doing research and more time trying to obtain support (money) to pay for it. Later, we contracted out most of our work and I spent most of my time monitoring these contracts. After I retired, I was able to form a small company called TECHNOCO (a contraction of technology and company) and continued this work for the government as a contractor until funding for Star Wars contracts ran out. TECHNOCO lasted for twelve years until 1996. I paid social security taxes in the form of self-employment taxes during these years. The six months that I was at Redstone doing temporary appointments, I paid social security taxes. These six months were counted toward both my civil service time and my social security retirement time. I started collecting a civil service retirement annuity at the beginning of 1985, when I was 55. I formed TECHNOCO at this time and was able to put as much as 25% of my gains into a company VIP IRA.

In 1995, when I was 65, I started drawing a social security annuity. With these two annuities and having my home nearly paid for, I was essentially independently wealthy. I also by now had an IRA where a considerable sum had accumulated, I have been and I still (2002) am yearly passing some of this surplus on to our children and grandchildren.

From 1959 until the spring of 1964, my job remained the same, that is, the same desk, the same lab and the same bosses, but I had been promoted twice. I was a GS 13. In this civilian Army, I was a first-three-grader, but this time I was not an enlisted man. My responsibilities had increased and I now had more people supporting me. I was now working in the new field of plasma physics and I was trying to make a discontinuous jump to the top of the learning curve, which I suppose never works. I built a high-energy plasma pinch machine and tried to solve the controlled nuclear fusion problem. It looked like this might be accomplished in the next one to five years. I wanted to be first and I did not have time to climb a learning curve. My experiments were a failure, but I learned that this problem is more difficult than anyone believed, especially me. It is now 2002 and the solution to this problem is still not in sight. However, many years later, I did receive a patent for producing a nuclear fusion chain reaction on a quite small scale. The issuance of this patent was written up in the Science Section of the New York Times and a copy of my picture accompanied it. However, this reaction was not quite controlled and uncontrolled H-bombs, even if they are small, are quite destructive and have few, if any applications. Another thing that I learned from this first project was that failures like this don't produce good research reports nor are they acceptable papers for publication in scientific journals. In my job we had to publish or perish, so I decided to take much smaller bites until I learned to chew better. That is, I was going to try to work my way up the learning curve. I started to look into developing diagnostic techniques that would help us to better understand plasmas. This worked well enough to get me recommended for a promotion to a GS-14. I was now making more money than I had ever hoped and this promotion would give me a considerable raise. However, I did not get promoted. The recommendation for my promotion was to be part of a package from the Personnel Office that was sent to the promotion committee for final selection. Since my recommendation did not reach the committee, I was not selected and I was not promoted. However, several research employees from my lab did get promoted. I felt that from our publication records (factor IV) that I should have been selected before most of them. I wondered if I thought too much of my work or of myself. The day after the promotions were announced, I was called to the Lab Director's Office. He apologized and promised that they would send my recommendation through as a single request and that I would be promoted next month. However, before this could happen, a hiring freeze was announced in preparation for a 15% reduction in force. About 5% of the reduction could be obtained by abolishing jobs that were not filled at the time, by attrition which was obtained by encouraging retirement and by other means. But 10% of the MICOM work force at Redstone would lose their jobs. We called this being out the gate. I tried to imagine what this might be like. To have a family and large financial obligations, be in a career position and lose your job. At best it meant that you could bump someone else in another part of the country out of their job and have to move. But then I was wondering about how someone else who had been bumped must have felt about losing their job. Somewhere the problem doesn't go away.

Fortunately, I would never have to gain the experience needed to really understand what this would be like. My job was safe; I was the only one on my register. The impact for me was that no one could be promoted until sometime after the reduction in force was completed and this might take a year or more. My lab director offered to send me back to school to complete the work for my Ph.D. at full pay plus enough per diem to at least pay for the move to and from the school of my choice. I don't know if this was the best ever (money wise) fellowship, but it must have been one of the best. I was making more money than some of my professors. This offer was to compensate me for missing my promotion. It more than compensated me. Given a choice, I would have taken this opportunity instead of a promotion. Without this, I would have never earned a Ph.D. Degree. This is just another example of how faith, not planning determined the course of my life. The only school in Dixie whose physics department offered a major in plasma physics was North Carolina State University. Dr. Willard Bennett, the man who had predicted the relativistic pinch effect headed their plasma physics lab, and although the plasma pinch was a different phenomenon, it too was first called the Bennett pinch. I called Bennett and he said that they would be delighted to have me. I applied, was accepted, and the government sent me TDY to North Caroline State for one year or nine months, whichever was necessary for me to complete the required course work, pass the qualifying exams, complete the residency requirement and have an acceptable thesis problem assigned. So in the spring of 1964, my family moved to a rented house in Raleigh, North Carolina near the school, which was near downtown.

By this time, my family consisted of a wife and two children. A son named Lawrence Dewey Roberts, born on 30 December 1960. Anne said that Larry was conceived in Gatlinburg, Tennessee, where I was giving a paper at an American Physical Society meeting. Lawrence was my father's middle name and Dewey was Anne's father's first name. But he was called Larry. We didn't choose Junior, because that was Anne's pet name for the family jewels. Larry was 6 lbs. 8 ozs. He was a small child and a little frail, but he was happy and a well behaved baby who went to sleep when told to, got up without complaining, and otherwise made life easy for his mother and therefore his father. This was not only appreciated but it was just what we needed. Anne's parents lived on the bank of a small lake called Lake Raymond, which was near Raymond, GA. This was my Camp David, where I could get away for a weekend or a few days to fish and for a little while, reduce all of my problems to whether the fish bite or not, and at Lake Raymond, they always did. To get to the lake, we would travel at night in our 1960 VW Beetle. We would place Larry in the well behind the back seat, which came to be called the back, back, back. He would go to sleep, sleep until we reached the lake, and get up happy when you woke him; play with his grandparents until Anne took him and put him in his bed. She would tell him to go to sleep and he would. Except for asking a lot of questions and talking all the time, once he learned how, this was typical of Larry's early behavior.

However, he was part of some unforgettable incidents. The first occurred when he was an infant and somehow one night he turned onto his back, burped up some milk strangled on it and by the time that we could get him to the emergency room he had turned purple. We must have been a sight; two adults in their sleepwear and robes with a purple baby and looking nearly scared to death.  They cleared his air passages, restored his breathing and his normal color returned.  After about three hours we were allowed to take him home.  There are unforgettable times in your life and this was surely one of those times.  Another time was just after Larry had been potty trained, which was at an early age, probably just after Regina was born.  At this time Larry was sleeping in his crib when he awoke because he had diarrhea.  He, the crib, and all of the linens were covered.  He was crying hysterically and saying over and over "Daddy, I no baby – I man".  I dug him out, took him to the tub, cleaned and calmed him while Anne cleaned everything else.  After explaining that he could not help it, that it was an accident, and we were still proud of him, there was no further problem.

We had a boy; Anne wanted a girl, Regina was born on 28 September 1962, and now we had everything.  She was named Regina (Queen) Anne (Queen) Roberts and as a young child and a young girl, she was a Queen.  She still is a Queen.  Regina really was a very good child, but Larry had prepared us to expect too much.  Regina was independent, stubborn, tenacious, and sometimes a little contrary, but only when compared to Larry.  Also compared to Larry she was quite and loving.  She was a "Daddy's Girl" and knew how to get her way except when she would butt heads with Anne.  When she was very young she would deliberately wait for an opportunity to do something that she knew she would be punished for.  When the chance came, she would do it with glee and take her punishment like a good trooper.  When we moved to Raleigh, Regina was about 17 months old and Larry was 39 months old.

The Clarks helped me move to Raleigh and nine months later they helped me move back.  I had much to accomplish in nine months and I had to overcome not being in the habit of studying.  I had been learning about one thing at a time and doing that at my own pace.  Now I had to cover several subjects at a time and complete them on schedule.  I had to learn again how to learn what the teachers wanted me to know and not try to understand a subject in any more depth.  Passing grades (B or better) were necessary and this is all that I tried to do, because I also had to pass a foreign language reading knowledge exam.  I already had credit for German, so I chose French and monitored a course in French.  This was a fortunate choice, because most of the scientific words are spelled the same in both languages. My main concern was passing the preliminaries. This set of tests that covered nearly all of the fields of physics was something like a right of passage, pass these tests and then do a good thesis project, defend your thesis work before a faculty committee and you would get your Ph.D. I was worried about the preliminaries, because this was a go or no go hurdle, and I needed to clear it on my first try. I don't know why but I felt that after this hurdle, hard work would see me through. Therefore, for me, I felt that the rest would be all down hill, but as you will see the hardest part would be trying to get to be allowed to start my thesis work. This is my most remarkable story.

The things that I was able to do before I could actually start my experimental thesis work included:

(a) Having the school agree that it would meet the academic requirements for a Ph.D.

(b) Having the Lab at Redstone let me do this work as the primary part of my job even if it took me years to do it, and assigning me one full time technician and access to the shops.

(c) Having the Defense Atomic Support Agency (DASA) agree that the results if successful would be a significant contribution to their program and to sponsor my work to the tune of $110K for the first year with follow-on work if the first year's results warranted.

(d) Having Dr. Tuck at Los Alamos evaluate my proposal and recommend to DASA that they fund it.

(e) Having Major Benvanesta the Air Force Contract Monitor at Aerospace Corporation to get the Air Force to pay for 30 days use of their flash x-ray Nuclear Effects Simulator, a 60K value.

(f) Having Physics International, the company who made the flash X-ray machine and where the machine was located, and who also owned the diode part of it, which was very expensive, to donate one diode for my use. That is, if I destroyed a diode, as one of their advisors said would happen, the work that I was going to do there would be over.

(g) Finally, having the Air Force send to the Army a written agreement to pay for the use of the flash X-ray machine.

Now I was ready to start my experiments. In the meantime, back at the
ranch (Redstone), I had built and tested my device for creating the plasma
column in which the relativistic electron beam from the flash X-ray machine
was to be transported and where according to theory, it should pinch itself.
During this same time my group had become interested in lasers. We were
interested in the C.W. Argon Laser when the $CO_2$ molecular laser broke on
the scene.  Electrically and mechanically this was a simple device similar
to a neon sign. We made what we believed was the third C.W. $CO_2$ laser
and the military's first one. At first we obtained 7 watts and by increasing
the length of the discharge, we obtained an output power of more than two
kilowatts. This was the world's first multi-kilowatt C.W. laser. This ac-
complishment was written up with photographs in the American Scientific
Magazine. This record was like that of Mark McGuire in that it did not last
long. Raytheon was also building one of these lasers, a folded one, and in a
very short time they had more power. Shortly after this much more power
was obtained from gas dynamic $CO_2$ lasers and the services were starting to
talk about laser weapons. For high average power lasers, this story is still
developing with chemical lasers in the lead. To learn how these began and
how and why they work see "Notes on Chemical Laser, Part I Background"
by Thomas G. Roberts..

This is enough about my work at Redstone. You can see that it was varied, interesting, and productive. This work produced hundreds of reports,
papers, publications, a few books and more than 70 patents.

In September of 1965, we were back in Huntsville, our house had been
rented for a year and there had been a fire in the kitchen, which did some
smoke damage, but when we moved back in, thanks to Merritt Clark, the
inside was like new. In Raleigh, Anne had done as much as possible to let
me have maximum time for study. She took care of the children, the house,
managed the finances, paid the bills and saw to it that none of my needs
went lacking. She also found time to accept a job. She designed and set
up a chemistry lab in a local insane asylum where the inmates who partici-

pated in special treatment programs would be tested to determine results. She was able to do this because she was allowed to set her own hours and much of the work like deciding what to order and ordering it could be done at home. The work in the asylum was done on weekends and during some evenings. These were the times that I got to spend with Larry and Regina.

My job now required much travel. Travel was necessary to get my thesis work blessed and funded. Travel was required to perform the experiments in San Leandro, California. Some of these trips were for as much as six weeks. There were also trips to present the results (papers) of the other work that was being performed in my group. I was now a Group Leader, but not a supervisor; that is, I did not have to do the administrative work. All of this travel made it difficult for Anne, who had to get by without help when I was gone. Anne had done such an admirable job managing the finances in Raleigh that she continued after we returned to Huntsville. But, for some reason, she reversed her performance and before I realized it, we were out of money and things like the mortgage were behind in payments. I resumed control of the finances and this remained my job from that time on. My need to travel continued and increased and later in life, Anne was able to go with me, which she especially enjoyed. Shortly after the first of 1967, I had completed all of the requirements for my Ph.D. I attended graduation ceremonies in May and was presented my degree. I was now Dr. Roberts. My mother was the proudest one there, and maybe she deserved to be.

Larry was now 6 years and 5 months and Regina was 4 years and 8 months old. About this time we (the whole family) became involved and then inundated with quarter midget racing. This was the most competitive and most time-consuming activity that I have ever been involved in. Larry and Regina were the drivers, I was the car and motor mechanic and Anne was the team owner and had to attend to everything else. This is the only outside activity that I ever let interfere with my job. For example, in the mid-sixties, I was running synthetic oil in the racecars. These oils were experimental, hard to find and expensive. Once the oil had been used and was contaminated, I would collect it, take it to my lab and try to develop ways to clean it and restore its lubricating properties. This was not part of what I was being paid to do. I justified the work to myself by thinking that if I could develop an economical cleaning process; I would patent it and assign the patent rights to the U. S. Government. My boss also knew what I was doing and did not disapprove. It wasn't long though before I realized that quick success was not going to be had, and this extracurricular activity ended. Larry and Regina were having great fun and Anne was enjoying the comradery that existed among the racing families. But for me trying to set up two motors for peak performance at each race was too demanding of my time. I had accumulated some very expensive high precision tools for this purpose and one day while I was in the new Service Merchandise Store on Memorial Parkway; someone stole my toolbox from inside my car. I took this act to be a message from my guardian angel and interpreted the message to be for me to change my ways. I sold both cars and made quarter midget racing a part of our family history. This gave me a tremendous feeling of relief.

While I was at West Point giving a talk at the Military Academy and Anne was in Atlanta at her mother's house with the children, Larry fell and broke his leg. Anne felt like she needed help and moral support. My airline ticket was through Atlanta to Huntsville. This flight was a special that week and it cost less than a ticket to Atlanta. When we reached Atlanta, they wanted to charge me extra to get off there. This did not make any sense to me, so I got off and told them to sue me. I never heard anything from the airline and that was that. I rode back to Huntsville with my family

My friends said that when people get to be a doctor they begin to think that they are better than other people. They begin to forget their friends and where they came from. Some say that they think that their "shit" no longer stinks. I told them that nothing like that would ever happen to me. They wanted to give me a graduation gift. I told them that I would like a nice name plate for my desk that said "Dr. Thomas G. Roberts, AA, BS, MS, Ph.D., L.D.D." When they wanted to know what the L.D.D. meant, I told them La De Da. I received a nameplate that says "Dr. Thomas G. Roberts, L.D.D." and I am still using it. I will know that I have changed when our, or for that matter other, small children stop thinking that I am their age and no longer want me to get down or come out and play with them. Anne said that nearly all children love me, because we are of the same mental age. If this is the case, I hope that I never grow up. I believe that the saddest moments in a person's life are, when his kids stop saying look at me, see what I can do and when he outlives one or more of his children. I pray that this never happens to me. I still have children and grandchildren that in their way, says look at me, watch what I can do. I am also fortunate to have a stepson, Tim McElyea who is much more than talented in the arts; he is gifted. Many gifted people have unfortunate lives; I hope that in the end he turns out to be the exception that proves the rule. All rules have exception, for example as a rule "if you don't use it you lose it", but of course, virginity is an exception.

In late 1970 or early 1971, a blessed event occurred in our family. We gained what turned out to be another daughter. It may be difficult for most families to understand how this happened. The basketball coach at Stone Junior High School also taught geometry. He was a fairly young man, who died when he was on the basketball court doing practice. At this time, qualified teachers, especially in technical subjects were in short supply. Anne had both a BS in Education and a MS in Chemistry. The Board of Education called her and got her to finish the math classes for that year. Later when Regina started to Kindergarten, Anne took a job teaching at Lee High School. After a year or so she transferred to Huntsville High as the, or one of the two chemistry teachers. She remained at HHS until she retired. Shortly after she started at HHS she had in her class a young girl, age 15, named Marcia Barber. She pronounced her name Marsha. We now pronounce it Mar-see-a. Marcia had two older sisters and all three had less than a desired family life. At this time, their father was an alcoholic, under treatment and her mother had to go to the hospital and may have died at that time. All three girls were, or had been in foster homes. Marcia's foster parents for job related reasons had to move to Florida. Because of her father's objection, Marcia could not be taken out of the state. School was closing for the day and Marcia had no place to go. Anne brought Marcia home with her. At Anne's insistence, we decided that she would stay with us until something more permanent could be arranged. I now had three children and to this day I still do. A relationship developed between Marcia, Larry, Regina, Anne and later myself, was like concrete that sets up slowly, but became harder and more permanent as time went on.

Our house on Mastin Lake Road suddenly became too small. We had to find a larger home and we sure did.  The house on Bentley Street was 3 ½ times larger.  Each of us had our own rooms, etc. and there was room for another family downstairs.  This downstairs apartment, I thought was one good reason for buying the place.  I felt that either my mother or one of Anne's parents would eventually have to live with us.  But as this time approached Anne let me know in no uncertain terms that mother was not moving in.  Anne was not only willing but encouraged everything that we could do for mother except bring her to Huntsville and taking care of her.  Any possible problem disappeared because mother true to her word, did not want to burden any of her children by living with them.  She preferred a nursing home if necessary and wanted her life to end in Savannah, GA.  After she went to a nice nursing home, as nursing home go, which was located at Tybee Island, we made fairly frequent trips to Savannah to check on her and see to her needs.  We also sent money and once took a used car so that my brothers, who still lived in Savannah, could afford to take care of her on at least a weekly basis.  This lot fell to my brother David and his wife Kay, who did nearly all of the work, which was a wonderful demonstration of devotion and love.  Anne and I both repeatedly gave thanks for Kay.  Mother lived until the end of 1991 and died a few days before she was 86 year old.  Mother lived about 29 years after daddy died and about a six years longer life span than his.

When we moved to Bentley Street, Regina was in the 5th grade and Larry was in the 6th grade at Jones Valley Elementary school.  Marcia was at Huntsville High school (HHS) where she was a rising sophomore.   Marcia had been living with us for a year or so and was rapidly becoming the big sister.  Larry and Regina loved her.  One day some people from the welfare department came to our house and said that it was not legal for Marcia to live with us, but they had no foster home for her at that time. They agreed to leave her with us while they try to find one.  Foster homes for 15 or 16 year old girls were difficult to find and my wife and children were upset that she might have to leave.  After a month or so the Welfare people asked us to be Marcia's foster parents until she became of age.  We were quite willing to agree, providing they agreed not to look to us for help again.  We figured that there were enough families so that one was more than a fair share.  From that day on, Marcia more and more became our child in nearly every sense of the work

When reaching high school, both Larry and Regina also went to HHS and each took Anne's chemistry courses. All three had played in the band in both elementary and Junior High school. This continued in high school where Larry and Regina were together for three years, until Larry graduated in 1979. Regina graduated in 1980.

The band at HHS seemed to be composed of three groups. There were the conformist, the non-conformist or quiet rebels, and a large group in the middle. Marcia and Regina was conformist of the type which society found most pleasing. Larry wound up among the non-conformist. He became involved with drug use to some extent and with sex at a much too early age. Anne and I were not observant enough to know what was going on until we had missed our chance to have an effective influence.

This is my story and not that of my children per se. I shall therefore refrain from trying to tell my side of their adventures in sex and the like except to say that Regina was unusual for her time. When she was married she was as pure as the driven snow. However, I must admit that Anne and I felt that we had failed Larry. You can't undo the past but you can start to affect the future and once I recognized my failure I have tried to be observant of Larry's problems and needs and to positively influence and help him.

Marcia finished high school where she had been the one of, or the one who marches in front of the band wearing a bathing suit like costume and twirling a baton. She was active in the Church of Christ and toured with a singing group of young people representing the church. She was popular and by this time she had a steady boyfriend – a high school sweetheart. After graduation we sent Marcia to the University of Alabama to continue her education. Her boyfriend, Brian Dale was sent by his parents to UGA. They managed to stay separated for one quarter and then decided to get married and try to continue to go to school with what help that they could get from the government and fellowships for the needy. Obviously it was not going to do any good to try to talk them out of it. So we pitched in and gave Marcia as big a wedding in her church as we could afford. I also gave them our extra (used) car for a wedding present. Marcia wore Anne's wedding dress and was positively beautiful.  After the wedding they both enrolled in UGA.  Brian wanted to become a preacher and Marcia wanted to become a nurse.  UGA was not strong in either of these fields so they transferred to Texas Christian University (TCU) in Fort Worth, Texas, which was a school of the Church of Christ.  They both managed to graduate at the same time, but not without mishap.  A son and our first grandson was born on 23 October 1978.  About six months later they took their first vacation and drove out to the Grand Canyon to camp out, but they did not take everything that they needed and Jeffrey Dale was conceived.  He was born on 8 March 1980.  After gradua-tion they both found jobs in Ft. Worth.  Brian had either changed his major from religion to psychology or his minor was in psychology.  Most of the jobs available in psychology were big on titles and small on pay, so Brian took a job with AVCO Finance Co. and Marcia became a nurse.  On 15 December 1981 their daughter and our first granddaughter, Bethany Dale was born. Brian soon began to feel that the practices of the finance work were incon-sistent with his religious training.  Marcia took a job in Birmingham, AL and Brian entered UAB to work toward an MS in hospital administration. After Brian graduated, they moved to the Atlanta, GA area where Brian got a job with one of the hospitals and Marcia entered Mercer University to get an advanced degree and become a midwife.  Marcia has delivered a nearly unnumbered amount of babies including Regina's first and helping with the other two.  Marcia and Brian should have been doing well financially, but ob-viously they did not manage well because they became almost hopelessly in debt.  We made an effort to fix this so that they had a good chance to get on their feet and stay there.  Nevertheless after 20 years of married life, nearly all of which were very good, or at least that's the way it seemed to Anne and me.  The marriage came apart.  Only Marcia and Brian really know why this happened.  Some contributing factors may have been that Marcia was a little older than Brian; Marcia made more money than Brian; he was a better cook than Marcia and Brian it seems, may have been having a case of delayed seven year itch.  Another thing is that, it may have seemed to Brian that the harder he worked the farther behind he got.  If this is true, I think that it was because he set his expectations too high.  He probably thought that he really should be doing better not worse than the Jones'.

Marcia was able to cope remarkably well after the divorce. At first it was devastating. The future seemed to be all uphill and the hill was quite steep and she felt alone. But with what help that she could get from Brian and with some help from her parents (us), her in-laws (Dottie Dale), in addition to what could be obtained from hard work and professional advancement, she has done and is doing remarkably well. We are very proud of her. After some years, Marcia remarried. She married a man named Dennis Harmon. He worked for Delta Airlines in Atlanta and had two children of his own. It seems to me that Marcia and Dennis really love each other and enjoy being together and doing things together. However, there may be a fatal flaw in their relationship. Their concepts of parenting are not only different, but they are irreconcilable. Betty, my current wife and I are able to make her kids and my kids our kids and to love each of them for what they are and address their needs without regard to who used to belong to whom. Marcia observed this and along with her experience of having become Larry and Regina's sister it made her want to try something like this. However, this concept or anything like it is not even conceivable to Dennis. His idea is you take care of yours without bothering me and I will do the same. This is something like the two independent families living together. It does not work. It wasn't long before each family had its own household, but the heads of the households remained married. When all of the children had left the nest, Marcia moved back in with Dennis, but this did not last long before some of the children could not make it on their own and moved back it. Again, two households were needed. Marcia is buying her own home. Daniel is through college, married and working, but so far no great grand kids are expected. Jeff has graduated from a two-year college and is trying to continue his education. Bethany is in college and is doing quite well. Dennis and Marcia are still married at least legally and I suppose they still see each other from time to time. The flaw in their marriage had so far not been lethal, but it sure has been detrimental, but not to Daniel, Jeff and Bethany, they seem to have been able to let these tribulations run off their backs like water off a ducks back. It remains to be seen if this marriage survives in any form.

Larry was not only part of the band, but he was also on the debate team. At debating he was very good. In retrospect, it seems to me that a good part of the debate team was left of the norm that is a non-conformist, which may have caused him to test some drugs. I can remember what peer pressure can do in a sudden way without anyone really saying anything. The debate team traveled a good deal and I am not sure that the supervision was as good as it might have been. In school Larry was not a good student. He, like I in CHS, made only those grades that kept him in the band and on the debate team. After graduation he wanted to go to Stanford University in Birmingham, AL. He chose this school because of its national reputation in debate. The semester that he was there, they had two teams that went to the national tournament. I received about four letters signed by the president telling me how proud they were of Larry's performance in debate. What these letters did not tell me was the Larry was missing most of his classes and was failing them. I did not send him back for another semester. Larry worked at several jobs including one at a foundry located on the Tennessee River. At this time he had good physical stamina and he was a hard worker. It wasn't long before he wanted to go back to school. This time he wanted to go to the University of Alabama at Tuscaloosa. I told him that if he would enter Calhoun University extension here in Huntsville, pay his own way for one quarter and make good grades, then I would give him the amount of money that he spent on Calhoun and send him to UA for a new start. He was happy with this. It fit his personal schedule very well. He went to Calhoun, made good grades and transferred to UA. Now Anne and I were very happy. We felt that Larry had turned the corner and was on his way. However, it turned out that he was intimately dating a high school senior who was going to UA after graduation and Larry wanted to be there with her. He was but his grades were not good enough for us to send him back the next year. After this Larry was back at first one job and then another. During this period Anne and I began to lose Larry again. He worked at several jobs including cooking Pizzas and helping to run Pizza parlors. He got one job with a company in Tennessee. They sold beef door to door. Larry would drive a freezer truck to Huntsville and go to homes where he had previously made an appointment. He would get some meat from his truck and prepare and serve a meal for the family. Then he would sell them as many packages for their freezer as he could by convincing them that the price he was charging was too good to last. Of course, he prepared a meal for us and sold us a load. The first steaks, those on top of the package were excellent, but the grade went down hill afterwards. Repeat sales were few and soon Larry had to find other work. Larry got discouraged and left home without telling us that he was leaving. I don't know what was bothering him; maybe he thought we did not love him enough. Nothing could have been further from the truth. We lost track of Larry for a while. I think that he left town with a girl. In any case, he wound up on a beach at San Diego, California, hungry and broke. At this time he did something that was completely out of character. He joined the Navy. When I learned of this, I was both happy and really afraid. I was afraid that Larry could not be regimented and I knew that he could not manipulate the military as easily as he had done us. However my fears may have been unfounded, because they never materialized and when Larry was discharged; it was honorable. I have this document in my files and every time I see it, I say to myself, thank you Larry. Larry's grandfather, Dewey Harbin only had daughters and granddaughters until Larry was born. Larry was the only grandson he ever had. This is the reason his name is Dewey. Until Larry was born Dewey had adopted me as the son he never had. When Larry was born, all of Dewey's pent-up admiration was transferred to Larry. Dewey was able to visit Larry in San Diego and see Larry in uniform and this was a high point in Dewey's and my life.

The day after Larry's enlistment was over and he had been discharged and while still in San Diego, he became very sick. He reported to the Naval Hospital for treatment and they told him that this hospital was for active duty personnel only. He contended that they should not have discharged him while he was in his present condition. They contended that he had an exit physical and passed it. He contended that although he may have passed, the examination failed. The head surgeon came and examined Larry and told the administrators to admit him to the hospital. They treated his symptoms for a week or more until he had recovered and then released him. They did not seem to know what had caused Larry's illness. In fact they did not know and it was many years before we learned what had happened to Larry. During this period Larry had repeated occurrences of the San Diego illness. He was losing weight, his endurance was decreasing, and his immune system was deteriorating. Something of an aids panic existed and Larry's problems made one wonder if this might be his problem. From time to time he would spend a week or so in the hospitals in Alabama, Tennessee and Georgia and he was in some of these more than once. Each time they treated his symptoms, which varied somewhat and released him. Each time they also tested him for aids. This was not his problem. All this time Larry tried to work and support himself, which became more and more difficult as his immune system became less effective and he became weaker. This went on until one December (about 1996) while staying at Marcia's in Atlanta he became extremely ill again. He was admitted to a hospital and they had him in the cardiac intensive care unit. His symptoms now seemed to be impending heart failure. My whole family feared the worst. A young doctor who was trained in endocrinology happened to see Larry. He recognized that Larry was suffering from Addison's disease. If you like, you may wish to skip the next paragraph which attempts to explain Addison's disease according to the dictionary.

Addison's disease is a destructive disease marked by deficient secretion of the adrenal cortical hormone and characterized by extreme weakness, loss of weight, low blood pressure, gastrointestinal disturbances, and brownish pigmentation of the skin and mucous membranes." The way that I understand it, is that the adrenal gland has two parts, an outer layer and an inner core. It is really two glands, one produced adrenaline as required by the nervous systems; the other produces steroid hormones. Addison's disease damages this part of the adrenal gland and these hormones are not produced or not produced in sufficient amounts. These hormones among other things regulate the osmotic properties of the kidneys. Without these hormones not only waste products (urine) are excreted but needed parts of the blood are also passed and the amount that the body retains is decreased. There is less blood for the heart to pump, which reduces the blood pressure, and fewer blood cells remain to help fight off infections and keep the body functioning properly.

The doctor told them to take Larry out of the coronary ICU and put him in a regular room and put him on antibiotic steroids. Larry started recovering and has been getting stronger ever since. Today he is in good shape, his endurance has returned.  He is able to work overtime when it is available,, and he can now whip me at most athletic activities except maybe in a dead lift competition.  The young doctor in Atlanta gave me the best Christmas present that I had ever received.  Since Larry was on his own, and had no assets, most of his medical expenses were charged off as welfare.  I told Larry that I did not want the doctor in Atlanta to go unpaid.  I wanted to pay him myself, but Larry said that he wanted to take care of this one.

Larry now uses antibiotic steroids like diabetic uses insulin and by doing so, he like a diabetic, can and does live a normal life.  Before his trip to the Atlanta Hospital, he had made a strong effort to get his act together and to try to prepare for the future.  With our help he had entered the Alabama Aviation Technical University located in Ozark, AL.  He was working on an AA Degree, certificates for air frame and power plant maintenance, and a pilot's license.  The recovery from the damage that Addison's disease had done, took two or three years.  To get by, he at first took jobs as available.  But he wanted to go to a school for bartenders.  It was something like a barber's college.  He learned to be a first-rate bartender and this helped him through his recovery.   On the job he learned that there are many men and some women who could run this country, much better than any of our presidents, especially the current one.  But unfortunately most of them are keeping bar.  Near the end of 1999, Larry married Lori Ann Graham of Moulton, AL.  He wanted to go back to the school in Ozark and try to finish what he had started many years ago in 1991.  Surprising to me, many of his old credits were still accepted at least at this school.  As a wedding present, Betty and I agreed to financially help him through school, but Lori would have to get a job while they were in Ozark.  She did and Larry worked as a bartender on weekends and evenings when his studies allowed.  Larry made it through school and passed the FAA test on his first try.  The Aviation Industry was doing well and jobs were plentiful.  Larry had joined the co-op program between the school and Warner Robbins AFB and had worked for one semester.  He had one foot in the door with the civil service, but he was considering which of the better paying jobs he might rather have when 9/11/01 happened.  This "war" on terrorism had begun.  The Aviation Industry was in shock and Larry could see that instead of hiring they were firing.  It seemed that he had worked so hard to get so close, only to suddenly find himself so far away. However, unlike the civil airlines, the military air services saw that its mission and its needs would increase. Right after 9/11/01 Larry called me and said Daddy, I think that I should take a job at Warner Robbins, what do you think? I said don't wait for them to call you. He called, got the job and is putting in as much overtime as he can. Maybe Larry now has a guardian angel like I do. If he does, I will bet that it is Anne. I don't know, but I believe at least for men all guardian angels are or were female. They took care of us when they were alive and maybe, if we deserve it, they don't stop.

Regina was only one year behind Larry in school, but in junior high and high school they ran in two different groups. No parents could ever ask for a better teenager than Regina. Larry, Regina, Anne and sometimes I attended Saint Thomas Episcopal Church. We were Episcopalians, which allowed us to drink. Episcopalians would say whenever three or more of us shall gather together there will always be a fifth. This was just a joke but it did emphasize a difference between us and most of our Baptist friends. Regina was also in the band from the fourth grade on. In HHS she was in the flag corps that performed in front of the marching band. One year she developed a bone spur on her heel beneath the Achilles tendon and even though this was very painful she refused to go through the operation to have it removed until the marching season was over. One summer Regina was chosen to be a member of the honors band that toured Europe and played at some stops that included the Vatican where they played for The Pope. The Pope rode up to the band in a golf-cart got out and walked along the front row, placing his hands on their heads and I guess blessed them. Regina was in the front row and being unselfish, as she was, she wished that she and one of her best friends who was a Catholic and was in the third row could have changed places. The group that Regina ran with was one of the nicest and most well behaved groups ever.

I believe that I loved all of my children for what they were and I never put pressure on them to become a physicist or a chemist or to enter any other technical field. I only wanted them to be able to carry their own weight, to not be a burden on society, and to enjoy life as best they could. Considering the difficulties they each have encountered, I am proud of them all six, and so far I am proud of my grandchildren, all thirteen of them. Never the less Regina turned out to be my technical person. She is like me in so many ways – in her other ways she is probably better - and she is my favorite. Things like this are a result of the integral of life and as you shall see Regina had many more opportunities to contribute positive differentials. Being a favorite does not mean that we do more for Regina than anyone else. Anne and I and now Betty and I do for or try to help our children as their needs require and our abilities allow. A favorite does not necessarily have the most needs. I hope and believe that none of our children would want it to be any other way.

After Regina finished high school she wanted to go to Auburn and major in physics. While she was in school she would come home on some week-ends ostensibly to get help with some problems that she and the boys were having difficulties solving. The boys (the other physics majors) paid for her trip (gas) because they wanted a new supply of jokes. Regina would not let me help her much. She wanted to learn on her own as she supposed that I had done. Regina entered Auburn in the fall of 1980 and in January of 1981 she met Kelly Kaaloha Carter. Kelly's father was an officer in the navy and Kelly was born in Honolulu, Hawaii in July of 1961. Hawaii had recently become a state and their first Lt. Governor was named Kaaloha. Kelly was named after him. Of course, they did not realize it then, but they were destined to become man and wife. They had a long friendship, more than four years where love seemed to have continually grown. Kelly finished school in March of 1984 and took a job at WJHO the Auburn Radio station so that he would be near Regina until she graduated in June of 1985. After graduation they came to Huntsville to be married. Sometime before this, Kelly in all seriousness formally asked me for permission to marry Regina. Regina, as Marcia had done, wore Anne's wedding dress and she was married in the same church building as Marcia. Girls truly are at the peak of their beauty on their wedding day.

After the wedding they moved temporarily to the Atlanta, GA area. Regina was accepted at Georgia Tech for their special master's program, which was designed to allow you to get your MS Degree in one year if you were a good student. She entered GA Tech in September 1985. During this year

Kelly got a job at one of Atlanta's hotels where he was concerned with their promotions of themselves (I think). That is, he worked to help put Regina through GA Tech. Regina received her MS Degree in the fall of 1986. They returned to Huntsville where Regina was to look for a job and work while Kelly entered the University of Alabama at Huntsville (UAH) to work toward a master's degree (MA) in computer sciences. I think that this used to be called business administration. By this time my company, TECHNOCO (a contraction of Technology and Company) had been in business for nearly two years. My office (more than 1000 ft. sq. including storage space) was also the Southeastern (US) office of Physical Dynamics (PD) whose home office was in LaJolla, CA. I was the Vice President for, I guess, the eastern half of the country. Physical Dynamics was part of a team of companies that constituted the SEDA team for part of the Ballistic Missile Defense Agencies Advanced Technology Center (BMDATC). The General Research Corporation (GRC) headed this team. I was considered to be the local expert on Neutral Particle Beam Weapon Systems and Lasers and their application to BMD. We were doing technology assessments. That is helping the government to monitor their contracts for BMD weapon developments. Regina could have taken a job with Kaman Sciences in Huntsville. However a wonderful thing happened, my work for PD increased and I needed to hire some help. I was able to talk Regina into taking a job with PD and working for (with) me.

Those who work the hardest don't necessarily have more good luck than those who don't work hard; it just seems that way because they are better prepared to take advantage of it. Time spent in preparation is seldom wasted. I had the pleasure of having my daughter working with me while my office was in my house where she was raised.

Kelly entered graduate school in Sept 1986 and graduated in Dec. 1988. He took a job with a company called List World. They were both working and felt that it was time for them to start a family. They felt that they had put this off long enough, but when they started trying, they found that Regina for some reason had trouble getting pregnant. However, by working hard, they did obtained success. Matthew Thomas Carter was born on 8 November 1990. The Thomas was after me.

As time passed, the TECHNOCO contracts, for its main efforts in support of various segments of the Star Wars Programs, changed from PD to GRC to Teledyne Brown to Nichols Research Corporation. Regina changed from working for Physical Dynamics to working for TECHNOCO. These funds began to decrease in 1993 after Clinton was elected President, and near the end of 1994 they were reduced to the point where Regina needed to look for work elsewhere. She took a job with the Huntsville School System teaching math and at this time (2002) she is still teaching. These years were some of my most cherished. Anne was at home. She had obtained an early retirement due to a disability. She was unable to stand on her feet long enough to teach her chemistry classes. Regina and Matthew with his nanny, Barbara, who was a truly wonderful person, were also with me, but not in the way. Never the less whenever I had a little time to spend or when I needed a break, I could go from my office to the other part of my house and play with Matt-man (Matthew). However, all good things come to an end and all too soon or so it seems. Only bad things seem to drag on forever. During this period, Anne was now able to travel with me and she got to go to England, Wales, Scotland, Ireland, France, Germany, Moscow, The Mediterranean, Canada, Mexico, Holland, Bermuda, the Virgin Islands, Japan, Hong Kong and other places including many parts of our own country. Most of these trips were working trips where I took extra time off so that we could enjoy the trip. Very few were cruises or tours. Generally we set our own agenda and did our own thing. In 1994 Anne had what seemed to be a minor heart attack. When she seemed to be fully recovered, I took her on a drive to West Palm Beach, Florida, where one of our dearest friends lived. We had planned to go down to Key West and return up the West Coast of Florida, stopping at Casey Key and places like that. We planned to stay in each place until we felt like moving on. However, after a few days in West Palm Beach, Anne started feeling a little ill. We decided not to take any chances and returned home. By the time we reached Huntsville, Anne was feeling fine, and some days later she returned from the beauty parlor still feeling fine. She sat on the couch downstairs and had a heart attack. I was not home. I was working at Space Defense Command that day. I went straight to the emergency room at Huntsville Hospital as soon as I got the news. I reached Anne while they were still trying to determine what had happened to her. At first they thought that it was not her heart because her hormone level had not been raised. They thought that it might have been her gall bladder or something like that. A little time passed which to me seemed like a long time before the results of the spectrum of her hormones showed that the hormone, which is produced when the heart is damaged, was very high. She was taken straight to the coronary care (ICU) and she died there. They knew that they could not operate on Anne but she got to feeling better due to the treatments that she was receiving. They thought that if they implanted a pacemaker that she would recover and we might have her home for Christmas. The pacemaker seemed to be working, and she was scheduled to be moved to a regular room. Just before she was supposed to be moved things started to get worse rapidly. Her heart started to seep blood, which became trapped between her heart and the membranes that enclosed it. Blood is incompressible so her heart gradually lost its ability to pump. Her blood pressure slowly dropped to zero. She died of congestive heart failure. I was holding her hand and she talked to me as long as she could. She did not seem to be having any pain and she seemed to understand what was happening. Even though, my families were at the hospital with me, I still somehow felt all alone. Matthew who had just turned four, sensed this and asked Regina to let him sleep with Granddaddy that night. This was just what I needed a lot of love and a little responsibility. Fortunately, TECHNOCO still had a subcontract with Nichols Research Corporation and a couple of consulting tasks. For me not only did life have to go on, but I had things that I had made obligations to do.

Regina looked after me. She tried to see that I ate well and fed me when she could me. After a while, friends like Charlie and Polly Cason invited me to "parties" where eligible women were also invited. I went to several of these parties before I decided that I did not want to meet any such women, not now and maybe not ever. I felt that I would never again be able to make the same kind of commitment that I made to Anne. To me, marriage is forever – meaning life. I believed that I would be a widower until I died. Sex is one thing, but marriage is much more. I really did not feel that I had it in me to make the required commitment again, and even if I did, where would I find a mate (not just a girl) who understood this and was willing to do the same.

I have failed to include a history of my health. I was a somewhat small thin child.  I remained this way until sometime after my first marriage.  At this time my pants were a loose 28-inch waist, with 32-inch legs.  Now the waist is 36 inches with the legs 29 inches.    For most of my life I weighed less than 125 pounds.  After I quit smoking, my weight increased to about 190 lbs.  Today I weigh 164 pounds.

When I was a child, I suffered from inadequate nutrition which was rampant in our neighborhood.  At the time, we knew nothing of the problem.  It was just a constant part of life.  Our main concern was to get enough to eat.  What we ate was a secondary concentration.  In addition to malnutrition, I had the normal childhood diseases of the day – mumps, measles, worms, tonsillitis, boils or carbuncles, colds, flues, pneumonia and from time to time something that we called the epizootic, because we did not know what caused it.  These cases should have been grouped together under the title GOK (God only knows).  This is not to imply that I was sick most of the time.  In fact, to me, just the opposite was true and until the time that smoking threatened to cause irreversible damage, I felt that my general health was good and that I would be able to walk, run and play indefinitely.  This was a prime example of self-delusion created by poor presence-of-mind and not being able to think ahead.

My first real problem resulted from poor personal hygiene.  The only time that I brushed by teeth was in the morning before breakfast and sometimes I forgot that.  In spite of this my baby teeth and adult teeth survived quite well.  I did not have a cavity until after I left the Air Force.  This cavity occurred in a wisdom tooth and before I had it attended to; it was, I think, bad enough to be pulled.  However, this may have been the cheapest thing that I could have done.  This lack of taking care of my teeth continued until I was more than forty years old.  By this time plaque had eaten part of my jawbone away, exposing the roots of my teeth.  Tony Duncan who worked with me recommended Dr. Baker, who was his Dentist.  Dr. Baker sent me to Dr. Reynolds to see if by working on my gums, we would be able to help me save my teeth. Dr. Baker wasn't going to fix them, if I was going to lose them anyway.  Dr. Reynolds said that he would try but if success was to be had, I would have to really work hard at keeping them clean for as long as I hoped to keep them.  After he operated on all of my gums, he sent me back to Dr.

Baker, who repaired by teeth. Baker's original work, along with all the work that he has done since then is still in place. I have the Hygienist in Reynolds Office clean my teeth 2 to 4 times a year. In between visits, I do work hard at taking care of my gums and teeth. They haven't deteriorated much since Reynolds first work. Reynolds has retired but his son is now a dentist and he has picked up where his father left off. I feel that I have a good chance of keeping all except possibly one, for the rest of my life. My wife, Betty does all that one can do to see that I don't fail to clean my teeth on schedule.

I have had three experiences that treated to limit my life or to severely change my life-style in a negative manner. One resulted from excessive smoking, one from arthritis and one from the effects of plaque building up and attempting to block my major arteries that supplies blood to the left side and back of my heart.

I started smoking in my early teens and even though I knew that it was a potentially lethal habit, I smoked until I was more than 40 years old. I enjoyed every minute of it when I was actually smoking. In my later smoking years when I was coughing and hacking up crud from my throat and lungs and having problems getting the day started, I changed my views about how statistics could not be applied to the individual, but only the group or set as a whole. This meant that some smokers would outlive most of the non-smokers. Even though I knew better (from my training in math and science) I thought that I would be in the long-lived wing of the distribution. One day when after walking up one flight of steps, and having to sit down and rest before I could go in and talk to my supervisor, I changed my mind about my place in this distribution. I felt that I might actually be on the other wing of the distribution! This day I decided that I had to quit smoking. I finally won this war, but the battles were long and difficult. It lasted nearly five years. At first, I tried to go cold turkey. This lasted less than a month and suddenly I was smoking more than before. Then I tried to taper off. This caused anxiety and interfered with my work and my ability to control my temper, which made me even more irritable, especially with my family and those that I loved. I tried cold turkey once more. I started when I had a partial pack of cigarettes with about 15 in it. I carried the pack for about 6 or 7 weeks without smoking. However, about 6 or 7 weeks later when I was back in

Savannah, GA for a short while and was fishing near the marsh grasses, a swarm of mosquitoes seemed to suddenly cover our rowboat. The others in the boat started smoking in self-defense. I took one of their "butts" and lit up. At first it made me have a coughing fit, but it wasn't long before I was enjoying it again. This was a huge setback and for a while I was smoking again at a very high rate. I knew that I had to have some kind of help, but what kind? I decided to try to improve my lungs by preventing smoke and therefore tars and nicotine from reaching my lungs while at the same time allowing nicotine to enter my circulatory system by absorption through my mucous membranes. That is, I would smoke but not inhale! I could not do this with cigarettes and I did not like chewing tobacco. Therefore cigars, snuff and things like that were out. The only thing left was a pipe. I bought a corn cob pipe and the cheapest tobacco that I could find. This worked because if I inhaled just a small amount, even by accident I would begin to have a coughing fit and have to stop smoking for quite a while. It wasn't long before I was able to smoke as much as I liked without inhaling, so I bought some good pipes and some very good tobacco, both of which were expensive. There is a definite difference between pipe smoke and that from cigarettes or cigars. The people who objected to other smoke went out of their way to tell me that they wish that everyone who had to smoke would smoke a pipe and use only the best tobacco. My lungs began to clear up. My lung capacity increased until after two or three years it was as good as I could remember it being. I could run, play tennis, softball, and golf or do aerobic exercises. However, smoking a pipe is a messy, if not nasty habit and after 4 or more years I became tired of cleaning pipes and cleaning up after myself. I was able to put the pipes away and walk away from tobacco forever. If I had not done so I don't believe that I would be here today. There are two lessons here; one is if you have not used tobacco, then never start. The other lesson is that if you do use tobacco in any form, then gather your strength and start to find a way to make yourself stronger than this demon. It may be the toughest battle that you will every have to wage, but you can win.

My next problem started when I hurt my left knee while running on a banked tract. When this sort of thing happened, I thought that you were supposed to walk it off, which is what I decided to try, but it did not work.

After staying off the knee for a while, I resumed by life without seeing a doctor. This incident started Arthritis deterioration in my left knee. After some time had passed, I began to have bad days with my left knee. This caused me to limp and to use my right knee too much, which started arthritis deterioration in my right knee. I did not know it, but this problem was inherited. Three of my four brothers and my father suffered this same affliction. Daddy learned to live with it. Herschell had one knee replaced and was going to have the other one replaced, but he died first. David is planning to have both of his replaced in about four months, after he becomes 65 and is entitled to Medicare Insurance. Johnny is the youngest and it is just one of the many problems that he has learned to live with. So far I also have been able to get by without having my knees replaced and at the moment I intend to try to do so as long as I can. Twice I have considered having the left knee replaced and once the right knee. The first time was near the end of 1990 when I got to the point where I could not even get into a car or van. My knee had become inflamed and severely swollen. This happened while Anne and I were on a trip to Florida. When we got back to Huntsville we went straight to see Dr. Phillips. He drained the knee, treated the inflammation and suggested that since my knee worked well as long as the inflammation was controlled, that we should see how well this would work before we attempt replacement. Replacement at this time did not have a long life expectancy, so I put off the replacement. A few years later, I hurt my right knee. There was a tear in what cartilage that remained. I had arthroscopic surgery to repair the cartilage. It wasn't long before there was no cartilage in either of my knee joints. Never the less, I was able to control the inflammation until near the end of the twentieth century when for a time I was not able to control the inflammation and could not walk well enough to play golf or go on trips with Betty. We had Dr. Phillips refer me to the Houston Clinic in Columbus, GA. My X-rays and I were examined at the Houston Clinic. The Doctor who examined my X-rays and me said that my X-rays were classic examples of knees that should be replaced. In fact the left knee should have been replaced 10 years ago. But after examining my knees, having me walk a little, asking about my golf handicap, and had me talk about one of our recent trips (the one to the 8 National Parks, I think.), he said "before Dr. Houston hired me to work at the

Clinic, he made sure that I understood that we do not treat X-rays; we treat patients." He said that there is risk involved with knee replacements and in my case; the gain was not all that great at the current time. He suggested that Betty and I return to Huntsville and give Dr. Phillips another chance to help me control the inflammation. We did and after trying different kinds and different combinations of anti-inflammatory drugs, we were able to bring it under control and keep it that way. However, if we again fail all I have to do is call the Houston Clinic and they will schedule a knee replacement on the next Tuesday or Thursday. At this time, I am doing better than I have in a long time, partly due to Betty's treatment with vitamins, herbs, nutrients, and love and seeing that I almost never miss taking my medications.

Due to the arthritic deterioration in my knees, it became progressively more difficult for me to walk. Consequently, I began to exercise less and less. I came to weigh more than 180 lbs and I was losing my strength. At this time, which must have been in the late 1980's, I was doing a fair amount of consulting work for SAIC where Betty, my current wife, was the Security Manager. My work was in support of Gene Roberson's Division. Gene was a Vice President. He had a large division which among other things evaluated the ability of other countries, like the USSR, China, and etc. to develop Directed Energy Weapons, such as lasers, particle beams, high power microwave and the like. I helped with this evaluation. I at times also tried to access how realistic our own efforts in these areas might be. Gene Roberson was also one of the world's strongest men. He in his youth had done the Olympic lifts, but at the time he was only competing in power lifting events, which included the squat, bench and dead lifts. I believe that was before his shoulder was injured, he either came close to or did lift a total of 2000 lbs for these three lifts. This may be difficult to believe, but in the mid-1990's, before he injured his hip which had to be replaced, he in four meets, squatted and dead lifted more than 700 lbs (around 750 lbs). In these meets his totals were less than 1900 lbs, because his shoulder injuries limited his bench to less than 400 lbs.

He not only was a power lifter, but he was also a strength trainer. He coached all SAIC employees that desired his help, for free. The only thing that he required of them was that they truly wanted to help themselves and were willing to work at obtaining their goals. He did not have a standard program. Each students program was different and depended on their personal goals. That is, why were they training and what did they want to accomplish? However, he was most interested in those whose goals could be reached through strength training. That is doing the power lifts as well as they could learn to do them. Of course, for those who wanted to run faster, run farther, jump higher (slam-dunk) or just be able to better enjoy life outside the gym, he had other programs like circuit training. Gene was not a big man. He made the above lifts when his weight was about 240 lbs. Gene is one of those people whose story should be told, but won't be told unless he does it himself. I feel that his story, like Gene himself, would be an inspiration to people who want to become and remain fit and who would enjoy being with and helping others to do the same.

In the late 1980's after I had retired, Gene saw that I had trouble walking and therefore wasn't getting proper exercise. His motto is even if you are handicapped or injured you should come on down to the gym and he will find a program that will help you cope better. I did and he put me on a strength-building program that would not only build muscle mass, but would also increase my bone density. After two years or so on this program I was able to compete in state and national power lifting contest and finish from 3rd to 1st place. Most of the first places came when I was the only one old enough to compete in my class. I won my first trophy before 1990 and by 1997 (the last time I competed) I had won 14 or more trophies. My best efforts were 340 lbs. in the dead lift, 315 lbs. in the Squat, and 195 lbs. in the bench. In my first meet, I injured my shoulder and now my bench is no more than 120 lbs. I can still dead lift more than 300 lbs. (305 in 2000, 2001 and 2002, both before and after my 73rd birthday). In 1995, shortly after Anne's death, I squatted 305 lbs. in a state meet. Today I would do well to squat 250 lbs.

I may compete again when I am in the 75–79 age group and if possible in the 80-84 age group. Currently, I work out three times a week. Twice I do circuit training or some other aerobic program and one day I squat, bench or do dead lifts. If I decide to compete I will go to a three or four day a week power training session for about 10 weeks before the meet. When one is training, as opposed to just working out, one should be as safe as possible. Whenever you are trying to increase your limits you are accepting some risk. Gene recognized this and we always have well trained spotters before we accept risk. During a training session in March of 1999, I was trying to set a personal record (PR) in the squat when I experienced ventricular tachycardia. This occurred when I was at the bottom of the squat and the first motion I made was not proper. Gene grabbed the weight and Bob Bell caught me and laid me down. I was not breathing and my heart had stopped beating. Gene, Bob and I had been trained in CPR. Bob started working on me while the ambulance was on its way. After no more than a minute or two Bob had my breathing and heart working properly. By the time the ambulance arrived, I was setting up and I am told that I was conscious, that I told Betty who was now in the gym to get back out of the way and let the people do their job. It is claimed that I told the paramedic that I could get up on this table if they would just get out of my way. However, I did not and do not remember any of this. The last thing that I remember was starting to go down with the weight to do the squat. The first thing that I remember after this was being wheeled into the Emergency Room of Huntsville Hospital. They examined me and scheduled me for a stress test the first thing the next day and sent me to a hospital room for a nights rest, I guess. I believe that they did a gamma-ray image (a movie) of my heart before I was sent to my room. The next morning I was taken to a room where stress tests were made. I was hooked up to a treadmill and was told to try to run, which was the last thing that I felt like trying to do. In just a few minutes, I could see on the heart monitor that my heart rate was becoming very abnormal. I stepped off the moving belt of the machine and heard someone say "grab him – he is in V-Tac again". Two men did grab me and place me on the table that was near the treadmill. I was conscious at this time. I heard Dr. Cox say quickly give him 50cc of (?????). The medic, who was giving me this shot, stopped and said this isn't the medicine which you called for. People were running around – not knowing what to do. All of this reminded me of what we used to call a Chinese fire drill. Someone said we don't have (?????). Dr. Cox said, get some. Some one else said, we can't, the pharmacy isn't open yet, but was supposed to be. While all of this was going on Dr. Cox was standing over me with an electrode in each hand. He was ready to shock me and this was the only thing that frightened me. The rest was like watching the Three Stooges. Things must have improved quickly because Dr. Cox calmed everyone and things became quite orderly. After being observed for a while, I was sent back to my room and I was scheduled for a catherization the next morning.

It is only proper that I point out at this time that the above description of my stress test is exactly as I remember it. However, it must be realized that I had much less control of my faculties than normal and Dr. Cox or anyone else in the room might remember the events quite differently.

I was conscious during the catheterization, but I felt no pain whatsoever. I could see on a TV monitor of what was taking place in my arteries. It wasn't long before Dr. Cox said, there it is! You have about a 75% blockage in the artery that supplies blood to the left side and back (or bottom) of your heart. (This amounted to a 50% blockage in the diameter). He said to me, we can put in a stint or we can do open heart surgery – which do you want? I said, surely you jest. He put in a stint. During June of 2000, I had a stress test and another x-ray image of my heart. This test indicated that everything was fine. This was done again in June of 2001. This time the stress test went very well, but the gamma ray image indicated that not enough blood was reaching the back of my heart. I told Dr. Cox that I thought that the image was not taken properly. My left arm was positioned so as to screen this part of my heart. He felt that the arm was not enough mass to produce this much screening. I wanted him to redo the image, but he said that this procedure was expensive and under these circumstances my insurance would not pay for another test. He also felt that even if another image was made and turned out somewhat different, there would be enough doubt to warrant a catheterization to obtain a definitive answer concerning my condition. These arguments made me realize that my wife and daughters would be satisfied with nothing less than a definitive answer, so I agreed to have the catheterization done. When I was done, it showed that I had no blockages and that my stint was performing very well.

According to my doctor, I was dead for a minute or so and several people have asked me if I saw any kind of a heavenly light or had some kind of an experience that would cause me to, say, become a better Christian. The answer is no. It was like a peaceful sleep and nothing more.

Since my heart attack, most of my workouts have been for my heart's health and much less for strength. The strength exercises that I do are to help me walk better for as long as I can. I have also been watching my diet (eating very little sugars and cutting back on carbs as much as is comfortable) and have been able to keep my weight down and my blood sugar under control. However, I do drink more. I don't drink excessively, but I do drink more regularly; generally at night before bedtime, something like taking medicine, and like medication, my drinking is expensive – good scotch or good cognac, a little good bourbon and very little beer. Gene Roberson and Bob Bell (Baptists) would not approve of this part of my regiment, but they do everything that they can to help me with the rest of it and for this I am truly grateful.

Well, maybe I now have two guardian angels because I met a beautiful young girl (age 59) that I had known of for 10 years. Her name was Betty Jo McElyea. She was a Mrs. Betty's husband, Gene, had died of cancer in 1991 and like me, she was not going to remarry just to be married. At this time I did not know that Betty was a widow. Betty was and is now the Security Manager for SAIC, a company for which I had been a consultant since 1985. Right after Anne died Betty told me about her experiences when Gene passed away and offered to help me with any problems that I may have with wills, insurance and the like. She didn't offer to, but she did help me through my period of adjustment. She did this just by being herself (nice) while we were at work. At this time I had some classified work that I could only do in a controlled area, the SAIC SCIF where Betty was in charge. Near the middle of February, I wished to thank her so on Valentines Day; I asked to take her to lunch. This may not seem like much but for me at this time, it was a big step and I guess that I made somewhat of a production of it. The luncheon went well and sometime later we went on our first date. We went to dinner and to the movie to see Forest Gump, then I took her home. So far we had only held hands, but I think that I did kiss her good night. After this date we began to see each other more and more frequently, both at work and after work. I came to know Betty better and better. The more I learned the more

I realized what a truly beautiful and sweet person she is. I was approaching 66 years young and suddenly I realized that I was wrong about wanting to live the rest of my life alone. The next thing that I realized was that I wanted to be with Betty for the rest of my life. So I said let's consider the possibility of getting married. I think that she felt as I did but she was hesitant. She was afraid that it was too soon after Anne's death. Not necessarily too soon for us, but too soon for my children.

To me getting married is something quite different from making it legal to live together. It is more like really becoming one unit. A unit that is made up of two parts that are equal in importance. When you are really married, you can honestly tell your mate that the three most important people in my life are "you, me and us".

When I first got married Anne and I had youth, health, and potential, born of preparation, for successfully competing in the society to which we were born. Materially we had little else – no money for an engagement ring or a honeymoon. The fruits of our competition were a home, children, their education, weddings, grandchildren, world travel, and savings for retirements and most of all happiness. Again happiness in wanting what you have. Death caused this unit to fission - destroying half and leaving half-alone and confused. Now with Betty, there was a chance through fusion to form a new unit. But now everything was different. This unit will not produce any children. We each had families and grandchildren for whom we feel responsible; and we had real estate, other investments and retirement assets for meeting these responsibilities.

I felt that the way to make this the best possible unit was to make our assets one and our responsibilities one and do everything together. This meant that her children, grandchildren and responsibilities would become my own and visa versa. This may seem like a "pipe" dream and to not be at all practical. For most people this is probably true. But I felt that Betty and I could be one of the exceptions that prove the rule (and so far it is working to as near perfection as can be expected of human participants). This also means that if one of us should pass away, the other would assume owner-ship of all the remaining responsibilities and try to meet them, as he or she believes the unit would have met them. Since Betty is the youngest and by far the best looking, this does not mean that she should not remarry if I were to pass away. Actually I feel that she should. The standards that she had set for herself for choosing a new husband were quite high. I don't really know how I slipped in under them. I am going to do everything that I can to cause her to raise these standards and to strengthen any weaknesses that might allow someone to again slip under them.

By July of 1995, even though Anne had only been dead for seven months, I felt that Betty and I were ready. Everything that I needed to consider had been considered and the pluses far out weighed the real negatives. The only negative that remained unresolved was Betty's feeling that my period of mourning might still be too short for my family to consider "respectable". I tried to talk to Anne about this. I did not get any feedback – at least not in English, but I knew in my heart that Anne would have wanted me to remarry whenever I really knew that it was right and not until that time. I finally convinced Betty of this and that by waiting we were only hurting and inconveniencing ourselves. She agreed and on 28 July 1995 we went to the Madison County Courthouse and obtained a certificate, that made it legal for us to try to form the kind of unit that represents the height of happiness – loving what you have and in so far as is possible doing everything together as a unit and accomplishing this by always thinking of the other one first. Unlike the case of nuclear fusion, where a very strong bond is explosively obtained; fusion in marriage occurs slowly and when done right, the bond can strengthen so as to be able to hold against all perturbations, even death. For example, Betty and I when it comes to the needs of our children and our desires for them, we ask ourselves in each case what would our previous mates have been proud of us doing now. Betty and I have been married for almost seven years and our bond has seemed to become unbreakable. However, we both sense that it is still getting stronger and may never stop growing. I truly believe that our behavior has made each of our children feel that we really are among the most fortunate of couples. Betty and I know it and know that, God willing, it will always be so.

# MORE ABOUT GOD

Let's talk about GOD and let's do it as logically as we can.

In the beginning there was GOD, and only GOD and nothing else.

GOD made everything out of what there was in the beginning. Therefore, GOD made everything out of itself. GOD is not a he or a she, GOD is, IT. Thus, everything is part of GOD and the sum of everything is GOD. In this sense, GOD is timeless. GOD is the ultimate conservation theory. So far, I like this. I am the son of GOD.

Some things are logical and useless or nearly useless. For example, my time independent law of location is; no matter where you have been or where you go, here you are. I hope to do better than this. For example, from the above we see that all there was, all there is and all there will be is GOD and beyond that there is nothing. GOD is the sum of everything or the sum of everything is GOD. Only GOD is timeless, everything else is ephemeral.

How did GOD make everything? He made everything, all living things and all non-living things from atoms. This is very obvious to me, but then how did he make the atoms? I will explain this, but I don't want to fall into the logical trap of trying to explain who made GOD and then having someone say well that's fine, but who made that which made GOD and etc. etc.

Let's begin with the protons, the neutrons and enough electrons to keep everything electrically neutral. I could have started with just the neutrons, but then I would have to explain where electrons came from. Later I will do this when I modify the current "Big Bang Theory" to correct it for the lack of anti-particles where the energy that created the big bang came from and why the universe is expanding at an accelerating rate.

For now let's note that all of the nuclei (plural for nucleus) are made up of nucleons. The simplest nuclei are that of the hydrogen atom which has one proton that is electrically neutralized by one external electron. The next atom is deuterium whose nuclei consist of one proton and one neutron. This is followed by tritium whose nuclei contain one proton and two neutrons. Atoms whose nuclei contain the same number of protons, but a different number of neutrons are called isotopes. Some of these isotopes are unstable. That is they are ephemeral in that after a time, called their half-life, half of them will have spontaneously decayed by ejecting one or more of their neutrons. The hydrogen isotope tritium is one of these isotopes. These nuclei (in fact all nuclei) are held together by at least two forces. One is called the strong force and the other is gravity. There is also one force which tries to push them apart. This force is the electrostatic force. The electro-static force is much greater than gravity. However, the strong force is much stronger than the electronic force, which explains why the nuclei are very stable. The strong force between proton and the neutron is called a nuclear bond. As far as I know the proton is the only thing that never seems to decay (sounds a little like GOD; doesn't it?). Before we get through, it will seem to be much more so. Also, the molecules are not completely electrical neutral which causes them to form only certain molecules and substances.

The main thing to learn here is that this is how GOD invented chemistry (the physics of the valance electrons) and that chance had nothing to do with it. It was done according to GODS directions. Chemistry as we know it is just our way of explaining how we understand and use these laws to explain our observations. You see GOD made all of the nuclei by forcing the nucleons close enough together for them to bond in a special way, such that the space just outside the nuclei causes the electrons to collect and remain in special places called orbits, so that the nucleus and these electron form the atoms which seem to be electrically neutral. I say seems to be because residual fields near the atoms are different for each atom.

Einstein said, "Everything should be made as simple as possible, but not more simple." This is Einstein's rule. I have been and I will continue to apply this rule even when I later explain at least one way that GOD might have used to start the "Big Bang". Einstein was wrong when he said that GOD does not play dice; GOD does play dice, however, he always uses loaded dice.

After GOD made the atoms, he utilized the atoms through chemistry to make everything that there is, both living things and non-living things. Again, none of these happened by chance.

Let's see how GOD made all living things. If you take all living things here on Earth and break them down into their basic elements, you would end up with one humongous pile of hydrogen, oxygen, carbon, and nitrogen plus some small traces of a few other essential elements. We can see from this that GOD created all living things when GOD invented hydro-carbon chemistry. The above pile is the dirt, dust or whatever, which GOD uses to make every living thing, either here or (I believe) anywhere else in the Universe. I believe that God's Laws are the same everywhere in space and time. Hydrogen-carbon chemistry is only one part of chemistry. Chemistry is part of physics. It is the physics of the valance electrons. Chemistry has the potential to explain every material thing that is known to exist outside the nuclei.

Since everything is GOD and beyond that there is nothing. Let's see where everything is. Is it concentrated in certain locations, or is it spread out all over the place? It turns out to be some of both. But it also turns out that nearly all of space is empty. That nearly all mass is concentrated in the nuclei of the atoms. The nuclei are so small that they fill an almost negligible part of the volume of an atom. Although, one nucleus is very light;. when you divide the mass by the volume, you will find that it is also unimaginably dense. The volume of the space enclosed by the valence electrons is extremely large when compared to that of the nucleus. All atoms are almost all space.

So far we have not used any numerical magnitude. When we do we will see that even the atoms are so small that it takes $6.02 \times 10^{26}$ atoms to make one gram molecular weight. For water this means that there are $6.02 \times 10^{26}$ molecules in one cubic centimeter of water and three times as many atoms. Yet the water is still nearly all space.

I may have to start using some data (numbers) in order to continue. We may need at least the following:

1 LB = 453.6 g (grams)

221 LB = 1000 g

1 OZ = 28.35 g

Our Earth = 6 x $10^{27}$ g

Our Sun =  2 x $10^{33}$ g

Our Sun = 3.33 x $10^5$ earths

Our Galaxy = $3.2^{10}$ x 44 g

Our Galaxy = 1.6 x $10^{11}$ Suns

Observable Universe = $10^{10}$ galaxies the size of our own.

Since there are 6.02 x $10^{26}$ molecules in one gram molecular weight of water (or any other substance), we can see that there are more atoms in one cubic centimeter of water than there are suns in our galaxy.  Plus (the suns in more that $10^9$) other galaxies.

I know that this is difficult to imagine much less comprehend; but since everything is GOD and beyond that there is nothing, we must realize that most of the substance of GOD is to be found where the mass is.  That is in the nuclei.  As I have implied above, I believe that God controls everything from these centers.  Inside these centers reside the forces which hold nuclei together.  We don't have to completely understand these forces; which is fortunate, because man may never completely understand them.  That would require us to get too close to it (GOD) for our own good.

However, we need to know and we can know how the residual forces which are extended beyond the surface of the nuclei, causes other kinds of atoms to be formed.  These forces are primarily positive electrostatic forces. These forces cause the electrons which are captured and are forced into certain orbits until the atom is nearly electrical neutral.  Since there electrons are in motion, they produce magnetic forces and these forces help to see that the orbits are properly filled.  There are also gravitational forces which as in the nuclei are essentially negligible because they are quite weak.  However, later we will see that gravity is the only force in the atom that extends to infinity and plays a major role in what happens at large distances.  However, at small distances outside the atoms themselves, there are residual electric forces that come from the fact that the atoms are not fully screened by the orbital electrons, especially the valance electrons.  These residual forces cause the atoms to form molecules which, themselves, are not fully neutralized which causes them to form substances, etc and etc.

None of these residual or bonding forces occur by chance.  They occur according to the will of GOD, and these processes continue until everything that has existed, does exist or will exist has been accomplished.  This includes all non-living things and all living things and these taken together are GOD.

Where do we go from here and how do we learn what is the best for us to be doing?  I feel that I have accomplished this for the near future and I have tried to explain it.  Our largest atom (as of 1970) is lawrenciums (a short lived radioactive element produced from californium) (LWD has 263 nucleons).  Atoms with nucleon numbers greater than 237 are unstable and are called artificial isotopes.  These nuclei also require only a very small portion of the total space of the atom.

What about the atoms that have a large number of electrons like 100 or more?  Because these nuclei contain a 100 or more positive charge, they pull the electron orbits closer to the nucleus and even though the other orbits are somewhat larger, they are much smaller than you might expect.  This is so because the successive orbits contain more and more electrons, all of the atoms are about the same size.

In my book, entitled "Rambling Thoughts", I started by trying to invent (create) a new GOD which could explain our reason for being or the meaning of it all, that is our (raison d'entre) justification for existence.  Parts, or all, of this book especially the appendix on the reworking of the "Big Bang" is included in this book as an appendix.

The Ancient Greeks are given much credit for the beginning of physics and if you understand what they did; I believe that you will agree.  For example Plato said that everything can be explained using three fundamental things that are not defined; they are just known.  First, there is matter and matter has to be somewhere, in fact, it is located in the void and since matter moves, there is time.  Time is that thing which GOD created to keep everything from happening at once.  Everything else is defined by using these three concepts.  One of the things that they defined or explained is the atoms.  They said that all pure matter, for example gold is made of gold atoms.  You can divide gold into two pieces, then four pieces and eight pieces and so on.  But not forever, eventually you reach a point where you can't split the atom and still have gold. For a long time it was believed that we could not split atoms and the Greeks definition was correct, but when I was in school, I was taught we did split atoms and the Greeks were wrong. What I was taught was not right? Because we did not split the atom, we destroyed it. So the Greeks were right, too. Let's see how much and how basics have changed. If we were to start from scratch to write a dictionary for the terms we use in physics, where would we start? How would we define the first word? Surprisingly enough we would and did start with three basic concepts that we do not define. These three things, we say we just know or understand and we know how to measure them. These three concepts are mass (matter), space (the void), and time; the same as the Greeks. However, we have greatly extended our knowledge of the concepts and how to use them. We define all of the terms in our equations so that the units of each term are some combination of mass, length and time. All of the terms in an equation are unit-wise proportional to each other. To make them equal (unit-wise) we use proportionality constants. For example, Einstein's Cosmological Constant has the units of time. It should be noted here that in classical physics equations, time is a parameter, but in relativity it is a coordinate. I see no need to continue this. Most of you probably decided this some time ago.

A brief summary of, or one of our important conclusions, is that nearly all of space is empty. The atoms, the molecules, and everything that GOD has created when taken together fill only a very small portion of the volume of the known universe. There are $10^{11}$ or more galaxies in the known universe and taken together they too fill only a small amount of the total space. However, taken together they constitute most of the mass in the universe. There is a great amount of light energy that has an equivalent mass and is part of the source density of the gravitational field. This along with the particles that are emitted by stars and other objects in the galaxies, some of which escape the galaxies and travel through the cosmos causes the space in and between the galaxies to be not empty. However, for most of this space, the density is only about one particle per cubic meter and this space is then nearly empty. There is in addition to the electron-magnetic energy mentioned above at each point in space, a gravitational force that is due to all mass in the universe. Even though gravity falls off as one over R-squared it is still not zero and each mass wherever it is contributes a non-zero amount at each point in the universe.

Unlike an ontological argument which is an a priori argument for the existence of GOD, asserting that as existence is a perfection, and as GOD is conceived of as the most perfect being, it follows that GOD must exist! But ontology itself is the branch of meta-physics that studies the nature of existence or being as such. However, I am going to avoid meta-physics by using a more simple logic, such as if A = B and B = C then A = C. It may be difficult to keep it this simple so I will just do my best. Let's start with:

- Every living thing dies,
- GOD does not die,
- GOD is not a living thing!

This does not say or mean that living things are not part of GOD. They as well as all non-living things are part of GOD. However, it does mean that every person, such as Alexander the Great, Jesus, and Pharos and all others who claimed or were claimed to be GOD, died. None of them were or will be GOD. GOD did not die; GOD cannot die. GOD is not a living thing. GOD is also not a non-living thing. In this sense GOD is timeless. GOD is at all times the sum of all things. It makes no sense to say GOD is dead or GOD is not dead. GOD is both dead and alive at the same time and it is as it was in the beginning, is now and forever shall be GOD without end. All there is, is GOD and beyond that there is nothing. This is a little like my time independent theory of location, which is no matter where you have been or where you go, here you are.

Note that all things both living and non-living things are made of non-living things. However, it does not follow from this that GOD will, at some-time, be only non-living things and therefore dead. To do this you must prove that along with entropy, everything will run down. This seems so in our solar system and maybe in our galaxy, but some seemingly dead things, like super novas, explode and produce solar systems where the conditions for life occurs and everything can recur or decease.

So far nothing has been said about religions. Religious thought is responsible to human society and not to any church whose orientation is humanistic, not divine. Churches and the like are all about wealth, property, power, control, self-importance and other material things desired by man. Even though you would think that this is difficult to hide, many of the Priests are trained to be magicians at camouflage. They are able to make you believe that all of this aggrandizement is done for the need of, or by direction of GOD. Even though, it is difficult to fit Jesus into this, the churches have done and are doing it very well. However, I suspect that it is becoming more and more difficult.

If GOD does not exist, nothing exists. We all know some things do exist. The statement that GOD does not exist is reduction to absurdity (reductio ad absurdum).

If I made my living by being part of a church, the above would cause me to pray every night and every morning as follows:

> "Lord never let anyone learn to prove that there is a personal GOD! If this were to happen there would no longer be a need for faith, churches, preachers and etc."

Religion is all about GOD and man's relationship with GOD. The churches and anything similar to churches are just the opposite of religion. Therefore, the phrase a religious church is an oxymoron. Enough said.

None of the above is to say that that man's religions are all bad, or do only bad things. Disregarding all of the people that they have killed in the name of GOD, we find that just the opposite is true. They have done and still do numerous good things, the most important of which was noticed by Voltaire who observed that they keep the poor from killing the rich. However, the churches are a very large part of the rich. He also said that for this reason, that if there is not a GOD, we would have to invent one. We would have to invent a new one because the existing GOD cannot be changed. To be so, we would have to change the churches dogma, which has been frozen in time for about 1600 years. Self-righteous is self-blinding. The leaders and the members of dogmatic religions are self-righteous because of their dogma requires it. This may be used to explain some of their faults. It is this blindness which prevents them from making changes for the better and it also illustrates why they cannot see evolution even though they are drowning in it. It is said that all rules have exceptions. For example, in physical training, the rule is if you don't use it you lose it. This is a very good rule, but it does not apply to virginity. Likewise, rules which have been created for or from dogma also have exceptions, but none will be admitted.

Before we turn to Rambling Thoughts, Let's consider for a moment Heaven and Hell. Wide is the gate and broad is the way that leads to destruction and many there be which enter there. But straight and narrow is the way which leadeth unto life, and few they be that use it. It looks like GOD made it easy for the bad to enter Hell and difficult for the good to enter Heaven. It sure looks like GOD could have done better and this only applies to Christians; all others have to use the easy way. Now when you consider the ratio of saved Christians to all of the other people in the world and especially if you include all of recorded time, it seems that the saved constitutes only a very small insignificant cult.

I do not want to continue this line of reasoning, because it only gets worse. Instead let's try to help keep the Christians out of Hell. Some of the Christian faiths believe in pre-destination. In order to do this, they have to believe that none of us (no one) has a free will. There is no way that we can contribute to our destination. This is blatantly ridiculous because –

• If there is no free will, then there is no Hell and we all are doing GOD's will! This is the one thing for which no one will be punished.

If we have to have a Heaven, and a Hell, let's use Zoroaster's. Here everyone except the Devil ends up in Heaven.

For the most part the above is concerned with the soul. I am not sure that I know what the soul is, but I feel a strong need for a human soul. If there is a soul, then wherever it is, it is like a point. It is in one place, and like a point it cannot be ripped apart. The human soul is therefore immortal. It cannot die. It is the part of GOD that is part of man and therefore part of all mankind.

Printed in the United States
by Baker & Taylor Publisher Services